Dr. Angela Douglas is the mother to three grown children and has worked as a School Principal for more than 20 years. After a traumatic accident, she re-evaluated her life and considered more deeply the road to health and happiness. Angela has extensive experience educating young people and is passionate about growing the next generation to be mentally healthy and happy people whilst also possessing the skills to live a fulfilling life. She is committed to having more fun, awe, meditation and kindness in her life.

Dr. Angela Douglas works with a range of different organisations to help leaders and others within the organisation to fulfil their potential, to inspire them to practice good mental health habits, engage in more fun and enjoy life a bit more which in turn leads to enhanced happiness and better productivity and morale. These are skills that are imperative to pass on to our younger generations which creates a more harmonious life and a next generation with improved mental health.

If you are interested in finding out how Angela might be able to work with your organisation, please visit *www.thehappyleader.com.au* or
Email: *angela@thehappyleader.com.au.*

Dedicated to Craig, Jack, Madelaine and Lachlan.

Dr. Angela Douglas

CATCHING PRESENCE –
AN ENDEAVOUR TOWARDS
INNER PEACE

AUSTIN MACAULEY PUBLISHERS™

LONDON · CAMBRIDGE · NEW YORK · SHARJAH

A CIP catalogue record for this title is available from the British Library.

ISBN 9781035821846 (Paperback)
ISBN 9781035821860 (ePub e-book)
ISBN 9781035821853 (Audiobook)

www.austinmacauley.co.uk

First Published 2024
Austin Macauley Publishers Ltd®
1 Canada Square
Canary Wharf
London
E14 5AA

Yesterday I was clever so I wanted to change the world,
today I am wise so I am changing myself.
– Rumi

Imagine if you could live your life with more peace, love, joy, awe, greater resilience and less stress. Would you want that for your children too? What if there was a way that you could have all of this plus more focus, better relationships and more creativity? Would you want to make the effort? The science is undeniable and the motivational stories are life-changing, but all of this does come at a cost. You will lose the ability to ruminate on negative thoughts, suffer less with anxiety, manage symptoms of depression more easily and make more friends.

I am talking about learning to live a more mindful life. I can hear you now ... *This doesn't work for me!, I can't control my thoughts, It is boring, I don't have time.* That's OK. You can choose to live the same way you have been for the past however many years, or you can commit to something better.

Learning to quieten our minds sounds very simple, but it is also very difficult. Meditation is not called a 'practice' for nothing! It takes time and commitment to change our way of being, but the effort will be worth it, I assure you...if you stick at it. It is free of financial cost and chemicals, but it will cost a small amount of time each day.

We are currently in the middle of a mental health crisis with medications on the increase for both adults and children especially in the western world. How did we get here? Can the simple but difficult practice of meditation turn this around? If the word mediation does not sit comfortably with you, call it something else. Call it sitting quietly if you like. Call it whatever inspires you to have another go!

My Personal Story

For most of my working career, I have held the position of primary school principal. For the past 20 years, I have found this role to be challenging, and I have lived my life in a constant state of stress. I put pressure on myself to make life easier for everyone in my workplace, as well as ensuring that each child in within my care was given every opportunity to succeed. I took everything personally, constantly ruminated over events and situations but had a very successful career with constant promotions. Since the age of 21, I have taken medication to lower my blood pressure as I lived in a constant state of stress and worry.

In 2011, I was the principal at a high performing primary school with an invested community and a staff who had been at the school for a very long time. I put a lot of pressure on myself, and on the staff, to achieve at high levels, which we did. Student academic data was the highest in the state, not just test results but improvement levels, general staff morale and parent satisfaction was at an all-time high.

However, it was one of those workplaces I found myself in where I just didn't gel with the other members of the administration team, in fact no-one gelled! There was a constant negative vibe or energy and I was always suspicious

9

of what was being discussed in my absence, but I persisted in trying my best to do a good job and build relationships.

In March of that year, I was invited to attend a fundraising ball for my former high school interstate. I saw this as an opportunity to reconnect with school mates and was excited to attend. The distance required a plane trip from Brisbane to Sydney, on which I enjoyed a couple of glasses of QANTAS red wine!

My elderly father had arranged to collect me from the airport. Somewhere along the way, Dad had lost some patience and it was well-known that he hated lining up for anything, so I knew that I needed to be in the front of the crowded pick-up area to ensure that his sense of humour was intact for the drive out to my childhood home. Another elderly gentleman was also collecting a loved one from this same area, which was under renovation. This gentleman pulled up to the boom gate to enter the pick-up area and accidentally put his foot on the accelerator rather than the brake, causing the car to plough through the boom gate.

This must have caused him great panic and distress and he attempted to correct his mistake. Suddenly, the wheels reached full left lock and he again slammed his foot on the accelerator, ramming his car into the crowd of people waiting to be collected. I was at the front and took the full force of the vehicle.

Medical experts constantly told me how lucky I was to be alive. I really didn't feel that lucky! I had three broken vertebrae and a brain injury. My recovery was painful, but I could walk! I suffered constant headaches and back pain. My doctors were great! They would constantly remind me how lucky I had been to escape death and major disability. Feeling supernatural, I decided that I would try to return to work on a part-time basis, because everyone obviously needed me … or so I thought.

Returning to work was difficult! I could not remember information from one day to the next. I would forget decisions that were made in meetings and was living with constant pain. Things then started to unravel. My doctor's visits would result in prescriptions for anti-depressant, anti-anxiety and pain-killing medications. This cocktail of drugs and an injured brain made it very difficult for me to interact with and lead people.

During this time, one or two members of my team decided that they would "troll" me as staff morale took a dive. Anonymous letters were sent to my employers and key community members indicating that I was a terrible leader and person. When complaints are anonymous, there is no way to address the issues with the person/s. I felt powerless, paranoid and defeated. My supervisors, I felt, just wanted to "keep the peace" at this high-profile school and encouraged me to take extended leave. I couldn't believe the allegations that were being made. I wracked my brain to try to find evidence of the person they were portraying me to be and came up empty.

I deeply self-reflected to try to make sense of the situation and grow from the experience, but I couldn't connect the dots. If the night of the accident was the last day of my life, I would have been very disappointed with how I had spent my last days. At that point in time, I was not doing a job that I loved, or living in the state of joy and happiness that I desired. Leaving was a relief!

For the first few months, I threw myself into my rehabilitation, but my husband, although very supportive of my decisions, was concerned about my long-term career choices as our financial life had been constructed around two wages and our three teenage children required financial support. I had also rewarded myself with a new luxury car. I was adamant that I was not returning to my job as a school principal ever again – a decision that was the source of much stress and many arguments.

My internal dialogue was, *I must be the worst leader in the history of the Department; I can't go back.* In hindsight this was not the reality as I had previously been the recipient of a "High Achieving Principal" award and numerous state and national media commendations. I was sponsored to travel internationally to share my PhD Thesis and had my fair share of positive feedback, but the positives are quickly forgotten. My internal and external world convinced me of a very different story. Once my paid leave ran out, financial stress added to my tale of self-loathing. On top of this, I had gained a substantial amount of weight as a result of my inability to exercise. My world was imploding.

I decided that my family would be better off without me as I found getting out of bed each day becoming more difficult and would look forward to taking the medications so that I could spend most of my time in an altered state. I believed that my gift to myself of my luxury car was what was causing a lot of financial stress, so I planned to drive it off a well-known cliff. On the day *it* was to happen, I waited until everyone had gone off to school or work and got into my car. As I sat in the carport and turned on the engine, I sat there for a few minutes. Then a song came on the radio by The Corrs: *Everybody hurts*. The lyrics are:

> *When your day is long*
> *And the night, and the night is yours alone*
> *When you think you've had enough of this life*
> *Well, hang on*
> *Don't let yourself go*
> *'Cause everybody cries*
> *And everybody hurts sometimes*
> *Sometimes everything is wrong...*
> *If you feel like letting go*
> *If you're sure you've had enough of this life*
> *Hang on*
> *'Cause everybody hurts sometimes*
> *Take comfort in your friends...*

Why was that song on the radio? Why did it come on at just that time?

I sat in the car for what seemed like hours and cried. I realised that I had let my external world and my internal thoughts and feelings destroy my life. I eventually decided that I was going to prove to my family that I could be successful at other things. I needed to convince my husband that I was worth sticking by and that things might not be perfect tomorrow, but I would prove my worth...And, I had so much to live for! I never told my family about my day.

Over the next four years, I experienced things I never would have had the chance to experience if I had not been hit by the car.

I owned a bar. It was a small venue for events which I ran with my two youngest children while they were studying at university. This proved to be very successful financially.

I tried to study acupuncture and Chinese medicine, however, this proved very difficult with a mild brain injury as I could not retain the required information and only completed the first year.

I helped out a mate and sold drugs… this was as a medical sales rep and the drug was flu vaccine! I also got myself a tattoo in Cambodia!

Perhaps the most transformative thing I did was to search for another way to heal and ultimately live. I had been in a place where I could not find inner peace and I realised that for me, this was more important than anything, and I searched for ways to find it and keep it. I also had to find out who I was as a person, without a title or high-profile career, and learn to love that person. I discovered many self-help books espousing affirmations and taking responsibility for both the positive and negative things in my life. I also discovered meditation. It all sounded so simple, but I quickly realised that it was difficult. It is known as a practice for a reason.

Try now for a few seconds to stop thinking… Unless you are an experienced meditator, you were probably unable to do this. We are wired to constantly think and observe the external stimuli in our world, but the trick is to actually find the still place within ourselves and get our internal state of being right. I am not suggesting that this will bring a perfect life, but it has been proven to have extraordinary effects on our brain and our physical and mental health which will be discussed further in this book.

Four years after I left my job, I was contacted to determine if I was going to return to the Department or resign. This decision was very difficult. The new Regional Director contacted me. She enquired as to my wellbeing and asked if I was ready to return. I had already decided that I was going to resign and find other opportunities to pursue.

The Regional Director then told me that she was not going to let me resign as I was a great leader and had a lot to offer. She apologised for how I had been treated by the previous Regional Director and the school "trolls". She wanted to right the wrong and asked that I return to the job. If I then chose to leave, it would be on my terms!

Well you can imagine how disarming that was. I had spent four years convincing myself that the "trolls" were right and I had been in the wrong career. I needed some time to evaluate her words and reconsider. It was the "safe" option and my husband was encouraging a return to this career path. I am very pleased that I returned as a school principal, however, I returned as a completely different person, and I wanted to see if my internal work had helped me to grow. I was also physically healed and pain free.

The mental health statistics of the Western world are shocking! Many people find themselves in a crisis at some time in their lives. My passion is to help others who may be a victim of their inner thoughts and external world to find that inner peace and understand that getting our internal world right is the key!

Chapter 1

Framing Resilience in Day-to-Day Life

As the days roll on and begin to blend into one another, maintaining a resilient mindset can become more and more challenging. Obligations and responsibilities stack on top of each other, and as you start to feel like "butter scraped over too much bread," it gets easy to overlook why we as people value a strong resolve in the first place.

Because to the one who endures go the spoils.

Through all your life trials, endurance will arguably predict your success as much as intelligence or wealth. No-one said life is easy, and it is up to you to make it worth it. That should inspire both a sense of freedom and dread simultaneously. Ultimately, it is *you* who makes the meaning of life's challenges. If you don't tell your own story, someone else will tell it for you.

The world will offer to you what it has, but you need to offer your sense of meaning back to it.
You make the meaning.

Resilience is what helps us cope and get through hard times. It can even make us stronger than we were before. When channelling resilience, perseverance and a sense of passion for the responsibilities you've taken on in life, ask yourself:

Yes, I am doing this for me. But who am I trying to be there for? Who am I trying to make proud? Who do I want to smile and hug and all the trials and tribulations and say, 'We made it? What would it look like if I could honestly say "I am in love with my life"?'

Now, hold on to that thought. All day. Let it be the last thought before bed and the first in the morning. That is a true, enduring meditative state which can contribute to building our resilience as we know there is a bigger picture at play.

Even in your speech, there are ways to frame resilience properly. A great playwright once said that words are "spells from our mouths"—and that saying holds a lot of truth. Think of how affected we all are by the words we hear every day. That's why we apparently all get "triggered" now. Whether we like it or not, words have a profound effect on our sensibilities and actions. To be resilient, you must speak resiliently—and mean it.

Here are a couple sayings that are simple and fairly generic but they give you a sense of how to maintain resiliency while wading through the waters of each day:

You may have to fight a battle more than once to win it.
                                            – Margaret Thatcher

Do not judge me by my success, judge me by how many times I fell down and got back up again.

– Nelson Mandela

Success is not final, failure is not fatal: It's the courage to continue that counts.

– Anon

I recently listened to a podcast by a young New Zealand woman named Tayla Clement. Tayla's story is a very powerful one. She was born with a physical condition that did not allow her to smile. She discusses the bullying she suffered as a child at school and the impact this had on her mental health. Tayla says she attempted to take her own life three times by the time she was 12 years old.

She talks about her journey to self-love and her acceptance of herself just the way she is. She was asked if she wished she was born without her condition, to which she responded that she would not change one thing about herself as she has learned to love all of her as she inspires so many others every day just by being herself. She is the true embodiment of resilience. She certainly understands the power of words and the impact these can have on others, both positive and negative.

How to View and Move Past Failure

If each of us aim to improve .1% every day, we will inevitably encounter failure. As you know, failure sucks – no argument there. But it's unhealthy to sweep the fear and feeling of failure under the rug.

Failure makes your heart beat fast, your skin crawl until you want to jump out of it, and the sense of humiliation may make you want to run and hide. NBA legend Magic Johnson famously did not leave his house all summer after losing in the NBA Finals to the Boston Celtics 1984. (Don't feel too bad – he won the next year!)

Failure can also be scary. It gives us the sense that we are not well-equipped or capable enough to solve the problem in front of us. Humans psychologically register the potentially severe implications of failure: not being able to solve the problem—in this life—could mean death. The fear can make you wide-eyed with disbelief and question your ability to survive, thrive and contribute to the world around you. It can be an overwhelming and crushing feeling.

You don't need to deny that quiet terror and desperation to move beyond your failures. In fact, it's best to take a moment and acknowledge the reality of failure so you don't run away from the first sight of adversity.

To illustrate the deep-seated psychological reaction to failure, it has been noted that in karate classes for children, some kids begin bawling suddenly and uncontrollably after being "choked out" in a grappling hold for the first time. It comes from the fact that the kids noted their safety was jeopardised, activated their "fight-or-flight" response... and still couldn't do anything about it.

On a deep level, the child recognises that they would not have been able to defend themselves if the altercation had happened in real life, instead of in the dojo. When it happens to kids in martial arts classes for the first time, the sensation is overwhelming. That's why it takes years of training to acknowledge—and then conquer—that fear of failure.

The irony, as I'll discuss in the next section, is that **only losers never fail.** Failure, taken with the right perspective, is a huge opportunity to gather information and awaken your senses. In fact, as long as you quiet your mind and open your thinking, **failure can spark profoundly positive shifts in attitude or behaviour at the fundamental level.** You don't even have to consciously try or overexert yourself! We as people are born with the ability to learn, and we maintain that capacity our entire lives. By acknowledging a failure, observing it, reflecting on it, and then moving forward, you will begin to make seemingly insignificant adjustments to your approach in life.

Over time—or all at once—you will notice there has been a remarkable transformation in your approach to daily life. This book is aimed to help you uncover the real you hiding beneath that fear of failure so you can be a light to those in your life.

Failure, like death, is an inevitability. It is the perspective you take on these failures, and how you leverage them to help you mature, that will end up defining you. If you fall down 8 times and stand up 9, you will ultimately be remembered for that 9th time you dared to rise up. If you struggle with anxious thoughts of failure, shortcomings or feelings of being 'less than good enough', remember the power of resilience. Endure. It will give you vitality on days it seems impossible to move forward.

Failure Proves You Aren't Just Going Through the Motions/Only Losers Never Fail

Yes, there are moments where failure indicates you are being lazy or absent-minded. However, failure often means that you pushed yourself beyond the normal "comfort boundaries" – beyond what you were able to accomplish the day before.

Losers never fail because they puff out their feathers and strut around when it doesn't matter, only to be *whacked* in the face by life when push comes to shove. It's easy to back away from something you are afraid of failing from. Humans are biologically wired to avoid pain and remember negative experiences more acutely than positive ones.

People in your life who offhandedly make remarks like, "You will never do that" or "That's a bad idea" or "that'll never work because…" are engaging in a cynical ploy – they dismiss your ideas and goals so they never have to confront their own. It's the old adage, "misery loves company" with a new twist. These individuals inflate their own lack of confidence by avoiding potential humiliation or vulnerability and instead act as if they already know everything they need to know. That way, if you do end up falling short of your goal, they can say, "See, I told you so! That's why I never tried in the first place; it was a waste a time."

The peanut gallery is filled with losers and those who avoid failure—or owning up to their mistakes—like the plague. For the most part, you can ignore them. These individuals are not worth your precious time, and arguing with them or giving them the light of day brings you further into a mud-slinging competition, and farther away from a place of whole-hearted successful living.

If a loved one or friend really believes you are making a poor decision, they will pull you aside in a much more thoughtful, personable manner. Even if they are direct in their criticism, it won't sound like some breathless "off-the-cuff" remark. It can help to follow the old Dr Seuss aphorism:

Be who you are, and say what you feel, because those who mind don't matter, and those who matter don't mind.

So, aim for success always, but do not run away from failure. Yes, failure in prehistoric times may have meant not eating or dying, but not every moment in modern life is governed by the "Law of the Jungle!" If it was, societies would look radically different in almost every conceivable manner. Running from pain in our modern world is a terrible idea that causes a host of unintended problems. It leaves you less equipped to deal with future challenges and can further entangle you in a life that centres on "avoiding pain" rather than "living free". Don't maximise comfort – maximise life!

True, lasting satisfaction comes from finding pain points of discomfort and building your resilience to them. The goal is to get more refreshing, revitalising "rest" in less time, while incrementally improving your capacity to handle the stressors, challenges, and adversity that come with pursuing excellence in daily life. Aim to maximise this "rest to effort" ratio the best you can every day without succumbing to the other extreme – burning out. This book does not promote a "corporate culture, work 'til you drop" ethos. When you are tired, rest. However, know you will sleep easier knowing you didn't lollygag and just "go through the motions". The purpose of life is not about waiting for the storm to pass, it's about learning to dance through the rain.

Exercise: Guess the Famous Person Based on Their Hardships and Failures

If you want proof that it is not failure that defines us, but how we respond to that failure, let's do an exercise. I am going to describe an individual, and you guess who it is below. You may be surprised by the results.

This person grew up in poverty in an American inner city. She wore dresses from burlap potato sacks and experienced molestation at the hands of her uncle, cousin and close family friend. She was raped at the age of 14, became pregnant, and suffered the trauma of a miscarriage. The horrible misfortune led to a relative impregnating her at 14 through forcible rape. Even worse, the little girl suffered the traumatic experience of a miscarriage afterward.

Now, there were rays of hope. Her grandmother would make corncob dolls and showed her deep, immense love. The young woman also demonstrated a knack for communications at college, perhaps angling for a career in TV.

But the adversity just refused to let up. She didn't finish her college degree with her peers. A producer told her she was "unfit" for TV – meaning he thought she wasn't pretty enough to hold the audience's attention. She was demoted. She ended up freebasing cocaine with her then-boyfriend, whom she had a co-dependent relationship with.

Plenty of justification to quit, right? You'd understand if, after hearing this harrowing tale, this individual ended up on the street, crazy and craving an angry fix. She had been molested, suffered a miscarriage, didn't graduate university, was shunned and demoted at work, and ended up in a toxic relationship abusing drugs. How should we view this person?

The woman I just described is Oprah Winfrey. Arguably the most famous TV show host in the world, now worth over $2.5 billion. Oprah experienced a cruel and traumatic childhood. She also felt the sting of failure when being told she was "unfit" for TV – a euphemism for, "You aren't a model-looking superstar and your personality doesn't fit the cookie-cutter mould people expect to see when they flip through the channels."

And thank God she didn't fit the mould. Oprah set the template for successful talk shows over the next four decades. If anyone has been defined more by her successes than her failures, look no further than the true queen of daytime TV.

Debunking Common Myths of Depression

It is important to talk about the realities and roots of depressive thoughts when discussing resilience and overcoming fear of failure. Mental illnesses cause suffering for hundreds of millions of people around the globe. However, the myths that have infected the discussion around mental illness are equally as pernicious and damaging – they may be distorting your perspective of discovering a proper solution!

The most important myth around the cause of depression is the most important myth to debunk first: the chemical imbalance myth. Pervading public discourse for decades, the "chemical imbalance" myth theorised that depression is caused by uneven levels of neurotransmitters in the brain – namely serotonin, dopamine, and norepinephrine. You've probably heard the names of these neurotransmitters or the "chemical imbalance" myth while talking with friends or family. Now, you can finally provide a more honest, helpful framework for these difficult discussions.

Make no mistake: the chemical imbalance theory is absolutely, unequivocally false. When it comes to building resilience and coming to grips with depressive thoughts, the chemical imbalance theory has arguably caused more damage to discussions around mental health than any other myth. While psychiatrists have not endorsed the "chemical imbalance" myth since the 1990s, the medical community also have not made a concerted, united effort to eliminate it from popular discourse. Instead, mental health experts have allowed this myth to linger, giving patients a horribly skewed picture of what is causing their depression and how to treat it.

In fact, Harvard Medical School released a study in 2020 illustrating that patients who discussed their mental illness using neuroscience terminology (e.g., dopamine, serotonin, biological and chemical imbalance) had worse treatment outcomes; it even predicted depressive symptoms following a treatment program.

Why? Because the chemical imbalance myth takes away the power of individuals to contend with their dark thoughts. Instead, it made them feel as if something was fundamentally wrong with their biochemistry that was completely out of their control. Naturally, taking a pill that affected this biochemistry would suddenly seem like the most obvious option. Unfortunately, doctors and psychiatrists do not seem to correct their patients' understanding often enough—or with enough force—to quash the chemical imbalance myth once and for all. Even if they had their patients' best interests on their mind, some doctors appear to not fully explain the fallacy of the "chemical imbalance myth" and go right to a pill.

An important note: if you are currently taking any anti-depressant medications, do not read this and stop them abruptly! Instead, consult with your physician and make it clear that you want to try tapering off neurotransmitter drugs to solve the root cause of your depression, rather than simply treating the symptoms. Antidepressant drugs *do* work for some people. But any honest clinician will tell you that medical experts do not know *why* antidepressants work. In fact, some doctors have described antidepressants as, in a sense, like throwing darts in the dark. You're bound to hit the bullseye after enough throws, but you don't exactly know how you found success. Still, this book recommends not completely taking antidepressant medications off the table while you look for ways to overcome fear, anxiety, depression, and build your resilience.

If you have been on antidepressants before and they failed you, have no fear – they do not work for nearly half the population. The side-effects can be debilitating. There are other treatments on the horizon—namely ketamine and psychedelics—but these treatments are still in the early phase of development. However, they have shown great promise in reducing the symptoms of severely depressed individuals.

In the meantime, it is important to give you back your power: depression is primarily caused by sad, devastating life events. Traumatic ones! But it's not due to some messed-up brain imbalance that is hard-wired into your biochemistry and completely out of your control. That is an absolute myth. If your depression is so severe that you are thinking of self-harm and worse, then anti-depressant medication may be a good option. Alternatively, the miracle is found in realising you can lift the veil of negative emotions from the ground-up by making positive, incremental changes to your behaviour that make you more resilient as a human being.

Mindfulness meditation, a strong awareness of your own sensibilities, and addressing poor behavioural patterns could lead to "eureka moments." Over time, you can wash over even the darkest depths of depression with your own light. Even if you end up deciding to take a modern pharmaceutical, remember the person powering whatever positive change you see is always you. It's always been you, and it will continue to be so.

If the thoughts of a traumatic event, or the anxiety of an upcoming one, come flooding to you all at once, it's ok. You don't have to snap your fingers and fix yourself all at once. Retreat and seek refuge in your quiet place. Enjoy the small activities and experiences you love the most – ones that don't have diminishing returns. These negative patterns of thought cannot be ignored but, at the same time, *they do not control you in the long run.*

Mindfulness means you do not run away from these past traumas, failures and fears. You also don't run headfirst into them! You observe them, acknowledge your humanity, and find solace in the environment you've chosen to build your resilience. When you can, retreat to that place. Build up your strength and remember that there is no chemical imbalance causing your pain, You are still here. They can be overcome. The magic is in how you realise your authentic self in the process of moving beyond these negative thought patterns and failure. There, you will find the unconditional love and enduring resilience you seek.

Do not overvalue positive emotions/experiences and undervalue negative ones

Being nice and overly positive all the time is severely overrated in modern society. It has gained the label "toxic positivity" and it defines individuals who throw out meaningless aphorisms like, "Positive vibes only!" These are the words of fools. Life is not one giant euphoric MDMA trip, and setting your expectations at "positive vibes only"—or something similar—will leave you unequipped to handle negative interactions or events. Why? Because false positivity encourages us to sweep real pressing issues under the rug, never contending with them or working through the stressors in reality.

Denying pain, poor conditions, or incompetence to remain "nice and positive" is as corrosive to your resiliency as constant complaining. This does not mean you have to become hyper-aggressive or hostile, shitting all over everyone who disagrees with you! However, trying to ignore problems by being irrationally positive will not work either.

Recently, Harvard scientists discovered a profound social effect labelled "positive relational energy". If you are a teacher, parent or mentor in some capacity, learning to harness this phenomenon has the potential to illuminate your life and the lives of those around you. It is important to note that individuals with high "positive relational energy" are not all hyper extroverts! Rather, they practice compassion, kindness and integrity, while acting with honesty and acknowledging the contributions of others through strong listening skills. By engaging in meaningful discussions with peers and loved ones, the positive relational energy has a chance to rub off, helping everyone better confront their fears and improve their resilience.

The Revolution Is Incremental

Take this as a simplified example of how your personal revolution is incremental in nature. If you improved, on aggregate just .1% a day for roughly three years, you could become 100% – *TWICE* the person you are now. That is 1/1000 of an improvement per day for a little under three years. If someone told you, "In three years, I can make you twice as powerful as you are now," would you take them up on it? It might sound less sexy when they break it up 1/1000 at a time! Why do you think college-aged students experience such a rapid growth in maturity from 18-22? They get four years of personal development along with education, incrementally building up their knowledge base and experience. That phenomenon does not have to stop. Be a lifelong learner, and learn to see failure as an opportunity to improve.

Put another way, most people tend to overestimate what we can accomplish in one year, and underestimate what we can accomplish in five. Your meditative practices should be geared toward encouraging that "long view" toward growth. When failing or feeling a sense of inadequacy, do not give into such doldrums! It means you are working right – your instincts have identified a place of improvement for you. You now know where you must focus your efforts to improve, instead of wandering aimlessly around in the dark.

Chapter 2

The Fundamentals (and Science Behind) Meditation

Sit, be still, and listen.
– Rumi

Meditation is How You Find Joy in the Process of Incremental Growth

By not being seduced by the "highest highs" of toxic positivity, nor giving into the "lowest lows" brought on by negative events, you will find yourself in a nice, even-keeled position to practice meaningful mindfulness meditation exercises. Meditation is important because, by bringing yourself to the present moment and enjoying what you are doing, how you are doing it and why you are doing it, the fruits of your incremental growth will start revealing themselves to you.

Remember! You are only here for a minute time. So, while you still breathe, adopt a sense of fascination with how every moment changes, yet seemingly stays the same. The passage of time becomes surreal, especially when holding a righteous amount of patience. Feel a sense of awe that you can even improve at anything at all. Without humanity, there would be only inertia – as far as we know. Without us, there wouldn't even be whispers in the wind.

Mindfulness Meditation Increases Neuroplasticity, Mood and Perception of Self

This book serves, primarily as a blueprint and guide for all of us to engage ourselves and our children in activities related to mindfulness meditation. In other words, teaching children how to seek refuge and find a safe place for themselves despite the tragedies they have witnessed.

However, to accomplish this goal, it would be prudent to first lay out *how* to access a genuine state of meditation as well as *why* mindfulness meditation can be so beneficial to practitioners.

The 'How' relates to nurturing a sense of resiliency and inducing a state of genuine awe (See more on that in the next section). For now, let's focus on the science-backed reasons *why mindfulness meditation could improve the lives of you and your children alike.*

Simply put, mindfulness meditation has shown, in study after study, its capacity to increase the density of grey matter in the brain – the structure that helps humans process information. Furthermore, meditation has shown that it can literally *change* key areas of the brain that control mood, decision-making and stress management: the Prefrontal Cortex (specifically the Posterior Cingulate Cortex), Amygdala (specifically the Left Temporoparietal Junction), and the Cerebellum. Some of mindfulness meditation's key benefits for the brain are listed below:

- Improved attention allocation
- Top-down and bottom-up processing
- Reward anticipation
- Decision-making
- Error detection
- Memory encoding
- Learning
- Self-awareness

(please check the sources – each publication has been cited by the medical community hundreds of thousands of times!) It will reinforce and serve as proof to you there is a profoundly positive good reason to engage you and your children in mindfulness meditation.

The Significance of Practicing Mindfulness Meditation: Improve You and Your Children's Lives

Parenthood is a heavy burden to bear. It turns carefree teenagers into anxious adults, and many struggle to maintain any sense of clarity while raising their child. Parents and teachers can get so caught up in the difficulties of their personal responsibilities that their stress bleeds into how they interact with their children – usually with problematic outcomes.

For example, imagine a married couple fought earlier over how they spend time together – one feels the other is not devoting enough quality time to their relationship. Ten minutes later, their child comes up to either the mother or father and asks, "Hey! Will you play with me?"

"ENOUGH! No, I am busy, entertain yourself," the adult snaps, fried and emotionally exhausted from the argument with their spouse earlier. Remember, the child has no context or grasp of the earlier fight – parents inaccurately believe shielding their children from real emotions (even their own) is somehow healthy. IT IS NOT. That does not mean you need to open up to the young child and say, "Hey, I need your contribution of the rent this month," but by trying to pretend that everything is fine and dandy, the child/parent relationship is harmed. The child walks away stunned (and a little frightened) by their parent snapping at them, even if it was brief. The parent half-justifies it by saying, "I'm just stressed" – but the child *is not aware of those external stressors. To them, you just hated them in that moment for some reason.* Over time, their willingness to engage with you as a child you love erodes, and children may begin to see through any parental façade you erect in an effort to "shield" them from difficult emotions.

Meditation can be a key technique to defuse these kinds of "mini-blow-ups" before they happen. Instead, when the child comes up to you after an argument or stressful event, you can just say, "Mommy/Daddy just had something difficult happen. Can I have 15-20 minutes of quiet time to meditate on it? Then I promise I'll come check in on you, and give you a hug while I'm at it."

During interpersonal engagements—especially with children—even one word added in the right (or wrong) tone can make a huge difference to the direction of a conversation. As a start to examining your patterns of communication, begin recognising the intonation you place on the first and last words of each sentence you speak aloud. Shifting the emphasis of your tone or volume on these words can lead to much more thoughtful—and even unexpected—breakthroughs.

Think of your voice like a musical instrument, because it is exactly that. Now, you are not singing, but imagine a trombone or piano that is playing softly, then suddenly hits a LOUD staccato at the end. Or, an aggressive, hostile-sounding guitar riff cools off into this quiet, almost melancholy melody. The volume and tone of your voice have the same impact on the individuals you interact with. Remember – these are spells from your mouth. It's not something to get cocky about; the people around you are affected by how you talk, down to the tonality of single words and phrases. A single word added, or tonality and volume shifted, can stir up an entirely different set of emotions when having a conversation. You'd do best to remember that next time you feel at an impasse with your partner, colleague, child, or student.

The Benefits of Meditation: Every Moment a Fresh Start

Do you feel like you screwed up something important today? Yesterday? Last month? A decade ago? As long as you are still breathing, meditation gives you a chance for a fresh start. Even if this moment felt overwhelming, meditation is a chance every day for a new beginning and a more thoughtful perspective on your issues.

Many adults live with traumas and past regrets. These past events only control your future if you do not offer yourself a new beginning. You may have crashed and burned in the past

– but you are standing today. You can still be the phoenix that rises from the ashes.

Sometimes, within these traumas, an individual may feel like an ice sculpture that was shattered on a hardwood floor. Even if all the pieces are picked up and taped back together, it is unlikely they'll ever be the same again. They'll always be missing a few pieces, or there will be clear breaks in the glass that makes it look ugly.

With mindfulness meditation, maybe you could consider a different kind of metaphor. Let's say you are, in fact, like an ice sculpture that shattered on the floor. No problem. You get swept up—every little piece—and transformed into an even more elegant sculpture by an artist practicing glassblowing. Maybe the experience makes your design all the more meaningful.

That is your meditation in a nutshell – a chance to pick yourself up off the floor, re-sculpt yourself, and become something new entirely. Change the metaphors you use to describe yourself – think outside of the box!

I want this book to dispel the veneer that meditation is this "always happy-go-lucky," "go with the flow" attitude. That is a misnomer and mischaracterisation of meditation. Meditation is a peaceful environment you create, so you are in the strongest position to face the most difficult feelings in your life.

Remember, many meditative practices derive their inspiration from Buddhist teachings. It stinks to be reminded of this, but Buddhism is based on a core guiding principle: "Life is suffering." Eek! Meditation is not some bubble-gum activity to breathlessly pontificate on with your friends. It's a deeply personal experience that brings you more in touch with your personal sentiments and emotions.

Martin Luther King once said that the point of his protests was to bring underlying tensions—racial ones in this case—to the surface. He stated:

We who engage in nonviolent direct action are not the creators of tension. We merely bring to the surface the hidden tension that is already alive.

It is the same idea with your consciousness. The tensions and stressors are already there. However, many individuals allow these tensions to stay pent-up with no release valve. Whether it's with the good intention of putting on a strong face, or through denial of a difficult reality, these tensions build up over time – until they burst. Then, instead of it being a minor discontent (e.g., an honest argument or minor course adjustment), the issue blows up like a volcano, causing all kinds of collateral damage and unintended consequences. It does not need to happen like this – adults do not need to suffer by repressing our emotions and true sentiments with one another. On the contrary, we crave the bond and connection that comes with sharing our biggest dreams, hardest challenges, and deepest fears.

Meditation is your mental detox – you may feel restless, anxious, or uncomfortable while performing the 15-20 minute exercise. This is by design! Your mind quiets for a minute, and all the most pressing issues on your psyche, and all the tension your body is holding onto, bubbles to the surface. From there, meditation and breathwork empowers you to dispel these pent-up feelings on a daily basis, instead of waiting until they give you a heart attack! That way, you are in a clearer headspace to speak sincerely and from your heart when the next difficult conversation comes up. Trust that if you are doing anything worthwhile, these difficult moments will come up.

So, brace yourself. Count on others, but be your own support as well.

Embrace Discomfort

A powerful technique to learn while meditating is that it's ok for you to feel discomfort, tied up in knots, when discussing difficult topics or situations. Your belly may quite literally feel like it's trying to run away from you—not pleasant. Learn to sit through these moments and endure them for a little longer than you are used to—.1% better than the day before.

After you know you've endured the limit before approaching "burnout" territory, provide yourself some refuge and solace with a simple, joyful activity that you consider one of your favourite things. Whether it's reading a book in the quiet of your bedroom (or at the park), listening to a new album from your favourite artist, watching a few episodes of your favourite TV show, or playing a game that sparks a feeling of genuine delight in you, do it for at least 20-30 minutes. This is your 'cool-off' after mentally enduring a challenging, uncomfortable situation. Give yourself that space and breathing room – your psyche will thank you!

Bathe in your refuge for a bit—so long as it is one that rejuvenates you—not one that makes you feel like you have to get away to avoid burning out. Feeling like you need to get away is an early sign of deep dissatisfaction with the structure of your daily life. Vacations, time off, and breaks are intended to rejuvenate your enthusiasm for daily living and engagements. If your refuge always leaves you craving just a little more time, it could be a sign of deeper trouble. A healthier response would sound something along the lines of, "Ahhhh… that was awesome… now, where was I? Oh yeah!" There, you are back in the pursuit of what ancient philosopher Aristotle coined, "The Good Life".

It's ok if you messed up – take personal responsibility. Sit in the discomfort for a minute as you go about your day. It's important. It's your senses telling you, "You can do better and improve this entire situation if you'd just learn the damn lesson!" So, learn it. You are capable. The fact that you feel discomfort at your shortcomings or challenging situations only proves two things in the moment:

1. You are not a sociopath (they cannot process emotions like shame, guilt, fear, or disappointment).
2. Your instincts are emitting this sentiment because you know *down to your core* there is some way to adjust your perspective, attitude, or behaviour that would improve the outcome for everyone involved (including yourself).

The Stillness of Good Decisions

It seems the best, most thoughtful decision-making comes during quiet contemplation. It may not even seem strenuous to you at that moment. Good decisions are simply the by-product of your instinct, intellect, and emotional clarity melding together to make sense of the world around you. It may seem spontaneous, self-evident, or almost too simple to observe. It makes you utter things like:

Could it really be that simple?
How did I not see it before?
All I did was sit back and observe the situation...

When our minds are racing, and stressors, feelings of guilt and anxiety become too overbearing, our judgement suffers. These are crucial moments. If you are reading this and are currently feeling overwhelmed—or have recently experienced such an emotion—be still. Catch yourself before you keep falling. The great writer Leo Tolstoy once wrote, "When in doubt, do nothing." If you are unsure of what decision to make, take one more breath. For now, do nothing, until your body and brain catch up with your restless spirit.

Consider this incredible fact: we only have a certain amount of decision-making power per day – about 35,000. Remember, this breaks down decisions to the smallest detail, "Should I walk with my left foot first or right? When should I eat? Should I accelerate on the freeway? What should I say to help my kids have better days?"

How do I make meaning of my life before I go, like a whisper in the wind?

Cherish your raw decision-making power; do not rush any one of those 35,000 decisions. It does not need to lag either, but... take a second to marvel at all the processing power you exert daily. There is a reason Artificial Intelligence, for all its supercomputing and chip complexity, cannot yet replicate human consciousness. It is because our ability to perceive and embody the world around us is a true marvel – a cosmic miracle. Let that decision-making power reveal itself to you through meditation. Until then, unless the situation calls for an instinctual response, do nothing. Show patience, and allow the revelations to come forth through the still quiet.

One more thing—you don't need all the information to make a decision—about 60 to 70% will do. Learn to rely on your instinct, intuition, emotional intelligence, and experience for the remaining per cent. Instinct preserves the value of your natural "autonomic" reaction. Intuition, on the other hand, is the human gift of foresight. It is the apex and synthesis of where human emotion and thought meet: the perfect balance of passion and rationality. Combined with your experience, you are equipped with everything you need to make the right decision. Endure through uncertainty, discomfort, and doubt until you find the answer you seek.

Slowing down does give you more time

When in doubt, do nothing. When feeling rushed, keep moving, but *slow down.* If you have 10 things to do, and you rush through all 10, maybe you falter on the 9th task. You end up being forced to redo it from the start. That "stop-and-start" motion may end up making you take as long as someone who steadily worked through each of the 10 tasks. The only difference is you feel fried like a piece of burnt toast, while the other person hums along, breezing by without overexerting themselves on small tasks.

Starting slow not only gives you a chance to do things right the first time. You train your "base" level of thought patterns and muscle memory with better consistency. Instead of feeling erratic and dishevelled while working, you slowly build up the confidence of your pace to "slow and steady." When rushing, you get no such luxury—all your energy and focus is to go, go, go! rather than, "Hmm... how can I keep doing this better?" A rushed mindset gives you no time nor space to improve as you handle your daily responsibilities.

Your children do not need you to move faster; they need you to listen actively and form a deeper connection with them. You are only a kid once, and even if you stay a kid at heart, we yearn to be listened to and acknowledged as children. It gives people confidence and self-worth as they age. By rushing, you may be missing out on these moments of active engagement because you are always superficially interacting, jumping from one task to the next. Rushing is important; the task is important. The relationship with your kids is more important. Keep your aim squarely on these values, and let time go by as it may.

At some point, what is slow and steady to you may look lightning-quick and efficient to others. This kind of accomplishment can only be achieved through natural talent or a great work ethic (sometimes a mix of both). Improvement may seem slow at first, and it probably is. Remember to focus on improving .1% a day – it's the best way to become twice the person you are a few years from now! (1000 days x .1% improvement a day = 100% better person.)

The point is, soon enough you gain a massive benefit through your deliberate clarity and thoughtful practice.

You do not need to obsess over every moment and movement – simply *be* there for them. We create bodily routines down to little mannerisms and changes in posture. Just becoming aware of those, slowing down, being patient, and fixing them will add up over time. If you normally slouch when you sit, take a breath, and rise to sit up straighter.

Changing your mindset during your routine and daily tasks, involves slowing down *just a bit,* giving your mind a chance to open up and explore ways to improve your approach. Time will not get away from you! After 15 minutes of mindfulness meditation, write down a few key notes as your "takeaway" to centre your thoughts, then *start slow.* The speeding up will happen naturally as you build momentum with whatever task is in front of you. You will only increase your stress burden by trying to go 0-100, and your ideas will fragment. Embrace the moment, start slow, and watch as you naturally begin to make adjustments. By moving too fast we can be perceived by others as having a "tick and flick" approach to relationships instead of slowing down and really being present for others.

When we walk like we are rushing, we print anxiety and sorrow on the earth. We have to walk in a way that we only print peace and serenity on the earth... Be aware of the contact between your feet and the earth. Walk as if you are kissing the earth with your feet.

– Thich Nhat Hanh

Reverse Effort

Another lesson to learn while practicing meditation is the wisdom of "reverse effort." Reverse effort is that sense that the harder you try to hold onto something, whether it be learning a skill or maintaining your child's discipline, the more it slips through your fingers.

You do not need to—nor should you—white-knuckle your way through parenthood. Trust your sense of clarity and alertness after practicing meditation.

You cannot force a child to listen to you, nor can you force yourself to deny emotions building in your chest. Reverse effort—inspired by the concept of Daoism's Wu Wei—relents to the fact there are forces in this world simply greater than our own individual powers. No-one can swim through a tsunami or resist the destruction of a hurricane.

Literary great Aldous Huxley remarked, "The harder we try with the conscious to do something, the less we shall succeed." Sometimes, being too overbearing in your personal engagements or "forcing it" bring little success to your efforts.

This may sound infuriating to read, but not all secrets of the world can be spoken out loud: you need to learn to try without trying. Crack that riddle, and life will bloom around you.

The Importance of Perspective: Peek around the pillar

While meditating, it is important to relax, let your mind widen outward, and consider perspectives that simply are not your own. Yes, we all have our own relative point of view! However, that is only one vantage point of billions: you likely have blind spots. We think the same thoughts as the day before therefore repeating the same patterns.

As a simple example, imagine you are in a large chamber with 8 pillars. You stand at one end and claim, "There is nothing behind any of these pillars. I can see that from here." Another individual, standing perpendicular to you, states, "No, there is a treasure chest hidden behind this one!"

You maintain, "No. From my point of view here, there is nothing behind that pillar. I don't need to move from here. I know there isn't anything there."

In that situation, all it would have taken for you to see the treasure was a willingness to walk over and observe the chamber of pillars from the other person's direction. Mentally, the same concept applies. There may be obstructions and blind spots from your point of view, but by never moving off your personal viewpoint, you simply may never see the value in shifting perspectives.

When meditating, picture your mind and thoughts doing this same activity. Do not stay in one place. Take your mind for a "walk" around the chamber of pillars. See what is behind your obstructions and blind spots

The crash course in Meditation

This following section is a "Crash course" meditation guide that relates to people who struggle with what to think—and how to feel—while sitting in quiet meditation. Hopefully, it's the most original, relatable description of meditation you've read in the 21st century.

The irony is that, with all the scientific proof and literature that has been written about it, mindfulness meditation still feels pointless on some level to many of us. The problem is, you may only be functioning at 80% of your full capacity because 20% of your mental capacity is tangled in a terrible stress knot.

Then, when something serious or important happens that calls for your attention, you suddenly feel overwhelmed – when you really shouldn't. You may accidentally lash out, or channel the culpability and frustration in the wrong direction. The 15 minute mindfulness meditation exercise presented here is intended to minimise the negative impact of these challenging situations. In doing so, you will notice significant, meaningful improvement in the following ways:

i.   Better clarity and focus
ii. Boosted confidence and self-belief
iii. Maintain positive momentum in your day, after working to establish it each morning

Handling parental responsibilities without 15 minutes of meditation is like playing a mental game of Twister *without ever resetting*. Yes, the human mind is miraculous, and it can make thousands of adjustments on the fly – even when stressed. But the responsibility of teachers, mentors, and parents is to put themselves in the best state of mind and body possible. That way, they are in the greatest position to set a good example, and inspire the children they work with. Mindfulness meditation is, for many parents and educators, the missing link for a harmonious mind-body-spirit connection. Do not underestimate its subtle power; the well-adjusted meditation places you in a position to be the person you know you can be. Set aside 15 minutes a day for it. A simple starting point. Now, instead of feeling "always one step behind," and finding yourself stressed and burnt-out in front of your kids or co-workers, you can be in a position to impress them with how you handle pressure under fire. The kids will notice when you feel stress – they may even find it justifiable. Still, they'll slowly develop a deep admiration for how, in situation after situation, you bring the same engaged, focused, present energy.

A final note: Deliberate mindfulness is different from taking a nap, distracting yourself or splaying out in front of your TV. Remember that distinction, so you don't confuse the two.

What to Think—and How to Feel About it—When Practicing Mindfulness Meditation

People don't know what to think about—and how to feel about that thought—when meditating. The disconnect likely comes from picturing a perfect, happy, little buddha as the paragon of enlightened meditation. This "Go with the flow, happy-go-lucky" image of meditation is an inaccurate portrayal of meaningful spiritual practice. So, when parents sit down to meditate themselves, they have about 30 seconds of saying:

"Good thoughts, breathe, breathe…"

Before the world, and all the challenges with it, come rushing back into their head.

"Right… breathe… I have to pick up the kids in 30 minutes. The youngest has a doctor's appointment tomorrow, but that's when the eldest's parent-teacher

conference is also. So... oh shit, I don't have time for this meditation crap; I need to go call the school and let them know I'll be late."

Educators may sit down after a class and go...

Ok...deep breaths ...wisdom... peace... unconditional love permeating the universe...

Shit. I don't love having to grade 100 papers by Friday though. And today's 3rd period was so fucking rowdy. Since when is it ok to stick 40 kids in a single class? I basically tell these kids the answers to the tests, and they still complain that I'm too hard on them? What, should I just give every kid a medal, an A+, and then fuck off until next Monday?

I wonder, am I going to get a new contract? I do love educating these kids and spending time with them. But what if one of these complaints blows out of proportion? Will I lose all I've built and worked for to get in front of these kids? I love being an educator, but this shit is so...

Phone rings

Oh, who's calling now? It's probably some parent telling me they're going to be late to the parent-teacher conference tomorrow. For crying out loud, how the hell are we supposed to communicate if you're not here? Ah, I guess I should pick up. Maybe there's a good reason.

(Or whatever your occupation; I am only drawing on what I know.)

Yeah, we know it really gets like that. Even for an impressive individual who juggles multiple responsibilities, that is a mind clogged up with layers and layers of unprocessed discontent. So, adhere to the tenets below when you get your 15 minutes of meditation:

i. Drop all Self-Identifying Labels, Presumptions, and Judgements of Yourself

When meditating, drop all labels and presumptions you have about yourself. That means no self-hating malice, nor any narcissistic justification of your attitude and behaviour. Meditation is *not* about judging your thoughts; it's about *having* thoughts organically float into your head, and honestly observing how they connect together to form your perceptions and presuppositions.

During meditation, think for yourself. You are not part of any group, association, or ideology while meditating. You are a unique, free-thinking mind among the 7.753 billion in the world. No-one has the exact stream of consciousness you are experiencing at that moment, and no-one feels the exact way you do about them at this point in time. Embrace this wholly individualistic (distinctive?) identity while meditating.

Do not start by saying to yourself, "Well, I identify with this group and this ideology and this political following, so that must mean I think…"

You'll be lying to yourself! Have unfiltered honest thoughts. Some of them will seem selfish. Some will feel rageful. Some will feel holy and sacred. Others will be boring and plain. You'll consider things that are embarrassing. Things that could inspire the world. New ideas that inspire yourself.

Let all considerations and hypotheses float by. You are not married to any of these thoughts. You are examining them and taking note of how they weigh on your consciousness

Are you a devout Christian? Drop the label for a minute – Jesus will appreciate your transcendental feeling. Who knows, maybe you even have a revelation about how to reach non-believers by stepping outside the paradigm yourself?

Are you a conservative, put off by all things "woke"? Bring down the defences for 15 minutes. Maybe then you will find a little sympathy, or at the very least be able to laugh off any absurdities in a good-natured way.

Are you a liberal? Drop the group identities, and be only yourself – nothing else.

Are you an atheistic or agonistic? Consider the miracle of many thoughts you can seemingly have at once, and how the world feels like it can move so slowly, when it is actually rotating at 1,670 kilometres per hour. Spark a little bit of awe in the perceptual world humans build up to get by.

ii.   Be Willing to "Ride" Micro-Moments

Micro-moments are instances where, mentally, you have one thought that excites you with a rush of positive emotion and, seemingly, the *very next second* counters that sentiment with some sense of doubt, insecurity, or anxiety about your future. Amazingly, the human mind can have 35-50 thoughts per minute: that's 50,000 to 70,000 thoughts per day. So, it makes sense that intuition can hit you one second, only for it to be blunted by a rush of subconscious counterarguments.

These flows of emotion can have clear-minded individuals feeling confident and "in control" of their powers one moment, and feeling desperate and "in over their head" the next. Fluctuations in emotions can be fascinating, exciting, terrifying, and overwhelming – sometimes all at once. Sometimes, when your mind begins racing and jumping to conclusions too quickly, you simply need to rest. However, when you feel able, endure through, keep your aim high, and maintain a steady pace. It will feel like a powerful release when your mind can roam free, running the gamut of your emotional range all in an instant. It's how musical performers or actors feel after getting off stage – it's everything at once. Very powerful sentiments are very powerful. Do your best to remember that.

iii. Breathe, feel, think – and uncover the indomitable spirit within you

Mindfulness meditation does not try and run away from the discomfort, nor does it judge the rationale for wanting to avoid pain. It acknowledges the reality of suffering while staying in the present moment. Soon enough, that sentiment can spark more light, remarking on the profundity of life as it happens before your very eyes. So, when meditating, hold in the back of your mind:

I am still here, I can uncover what makes me indomitable.
I am still here, I can discover what makes me indomitable.

Not only will your own quality of life increase, and not only will you bring more ingenuity to solving personal problems, but your ability to connect and bond to students and children will increase immeasurably. They will admire—and be drawn to—your improved ability to handle the adversity of daily life.

So, what is meditation? In a phrase, meditation is the practice of uncovering your indomitable spirit.

The 15-minute drill – making meditation work with your busiest days

Before you do something routine, important, or an activity you consider exhausting, plan for 15 minutes in front of that time. Get into a comfortable position, which can be lying down, sitting, or even going for a "walking meditation!" Just make sure the practice of quiet mindfulness is the deliberate aim of those 15 minutes. The world will be here when you get back, but it needs you at your best – so cherish these moments to yourself. They will likely become the moments where you have your best ideas of the day.

While meditating, relax every muscle in your body, specifically focusing on your shoulders, neck, and torso—all the way out to your fingers and down to your toes. Unfurrow your brow, and make sure your eyes are calm—your jaw unclenched. Tilt your head up slowly, and straighten out your shoulders. They should be aligned with your ears. Begin breathing with a calm, natural rhythm. At the beginning, some breaths may be deep, others shallow. As long as you maintain the aim of balanced breathwork, your inhales and exhales will equalise after a few minutes.

Let your mind wander before easing back into your chosen refrain of mantra for the day. Some ideas for daily mantras are found below:

Endure today for the victory tomorrow.

My past shortcomings do not have to define today. Today defines today.

Fall down 7 times, stand up 8.

Show up. Stay consistent. Stay balanced. And follow through all the way

Push myself, then rest. Push myself, then rest.

All hail me for having the courage of original/individual thought

I will live my own life, because only I will die my own death.

Let meditation be a time of divergent thinking – many possible solutions at once. When back to a more particular focus, you can then hone those divergent thoughts with convergent thinking, providing comfortable routine and balance as a counterpoint to the expansive, wandering thoughts experienced during meditation. The "15 minutes of mindfulness" meditation practice described above enhances self-awareness, flow of thought, sense of self, clarity, and perspective while you engage your children, colleagues, friends, and loved ones.

Move slowly after your 15 minutes of meditation, and jot down the major ideas of what came to mind. You'll be able to better examine the mental patterns of your daily thinking. It may shock you how often you repeat a very similar pattern of thinking, even though, in the moment, you are totally unaware of your routinised approach to each situation. At the same time, put a lock on this journal. When you are sorting out who you really are with mindfulness meditation, keep your most sacred thoughts private. It can be a dirty world out here, and you'll want to keep some of your inner feelings untainted by it for the time being. You don't have to post your every thought and feeling and opinion on social media – save some for yourself. It'll give you your own sense of mystique, something very powerful, and often lost on the modern world. The goal is that the magic of some of these sentiments transmit through the air, and you will not be forced to utter the thoughts you hold dearest until the time is right. Remember, only speak when something needs to be said – not when you feel the need to say something.

Keep a Yin-Yang Diary When Angry to the Point of Bursting

Many adults end up feeling frustration, resentment, anger, disappointment, and even pure rage at key moments in our life. It may be directed at our significant other, a boss, a dear friend, some random bloke... even your own children! Nothing is more deflating than a well-intentioned parent or teacher fraying their relationship with their kids because they snapped in a moment of stress.

The truth is that these intense, rage-filled demotions have a seductive allure to them. That's where the image of a devil on our shoulder saying, "Do it, do it, do it!" comes from. Mindfulness meditation is here to help the better angels of your nature win out. In reality, this kind of indignant outrage does, in fact, make for a quick self-righteous high. However, it ends up feeling quite pedestrian in the following moments, leaving you potentially worse-off than before.

Instead of trying to suppress your frustration or letting it boil out of control, do this: **write down whatever is**

bothering you so deeply. Return to that note multiple times a day to add the other parts that get you so upset. This is the "yin" part of your diary, so label it as such. A Yin-Yang Diary can help you figure out what really bothered you about the interaction, giving you an outlet free from outside interference. The objective is to distil the source of your frustration—over a specific situation or individual—into a single sentence or idea. That way, the oblique source of your rage become something tangible, a notion you can actually contend with and overcome.

Without purifying the true essence of what got you so upset, the justification of your rage will seemingly shapeshift. It seems impossible to pin down because you have not used your words to define the roots of your discontent with accuracy and honesty. Your mind will continue racing, flush with frustration, until you make sense of the situation with your words – express your sentiments in full.

For this private Yin-Yang Diary exercise to succeed, you need to write down and express the intensity of your emotions in the most intimate, vulnerable, and cathartic way possible. DO NOT SHARE THESE UNFILTERED THOUGHTS OF FURY WITH ANYONE! And do not approach the target of your ire prematurely. This exercise is to vent true feelings of rage, but just because your feelings are valid it does not mean they should drive and justify your behaviour in every unpleasant or uncomfortable interaction.

You may frighten even yourself—or be disappointed—in the pettiness, viciousness, and visceral negativity of some of the things you write down. Simply make sure the message is under lock and key – it is not how you *really* feel about the situation or the individual. This exercise is not to justify your hatred for someone or something. Quite the opposite, in fact. It is to expel these feelings of resentment and revenge so they stop affecting your judgement and ruining your days. A successful "Diary of Fury" is a cathartic release of confusion, frustration, and anger, not some list of petty grievances about all the people who have wronged you. In other words, when writing down these red-hot feelings, you are only transcribing one side of the coin: the "Yin" side.

With the rage purged from your conscious, however, you can let some of your troubled thoughts go. Gradually, ideas of why you love and care so much (about the situation) float back into your conscious – the "Yang" side of your conscious. When done in the right spirit, your mind will likely have a "yin-yang" effect, providing you a more righteous, beautiful, loving counterpoint to the raw anger you expressed in your Diary of Fury. These sudden feelings of contrite forgiveness, more measured thinking, and desire to rise above the discontent (or disagreement) will be triggered by the rage and injustice you felt while writing the previous message. It is almost a form of "call-response" from different parts of your mind. Your mind will balance it out naturally: the yin, being the darkness of your anger and the yang, your light shining through. In this case, let the light win out. There is a righteous way forward through your discontent. The duality of the Yin-Yang Diary is a powerful extension of your new mindfulness meditation routine. Guard it well.

While you work through challenging emotions in your Yin-Yang Diary, observe yourself, and see if the level of incensed emotion you transcribe melts away. If it does, wonderful – time to move on. If it does not, you may need to say something, or engage with the source of your ire. When doing so, remember that being *nice* can be overrated, while being *kind* is not. Confrontation can be tense. It can feel like a negative experience to many, but truly great parents and teachers know how to deliver hard truths. Do not be afraid of confrontation, but don't go looking for it either. Avoid "egging yourself on," like the devil on your shoulder would. If you want a better life for yourself, and for those around, and for your unsettled feelings to one day truly resolve themselves, opt for the better angels of your nature. This, one might argue, is the true illustration of enlightenment: acknowledging the suffering, resentment, tragedy, and rage one personally feels while moving through the world. And yet, they still opt for the better angels of their nature in every situation.

Rest When You Are Tired

Sometimes our modern work culture celebrates the idea of never resting and never accepting help. While the message, "Don't give up. Don't ever give up," resonates loud, there is another message—equally as powerful—that helps bear the burden we all face:

> *Live. Live. Fight like hell. And when you get too tired to fight, then lay down and rest and let somebody else fight for you. That's also very, very important. I can't do this "Don't Give up thing" all by myself.*
>
> – Stuart Scott

Famous ESPN broadcaster, Stuart Scott, said these words six months before his passing from stage IV cancer, while speaking at the ESPYs award show. Although he had achieved the pinnacle of success in a highly-competitive environment, like sports and entertainment, Stuart Scott reminded the audience that running until you simply burn out is not good for anyone. Take these words to heart while you succeed and struggle through every moment of the day. Fight. Push back. Exert yourself fully. But when you are tired, there is no shame in showing vulnerability, opening up, and resting. Your loved ones can fight for you while you rest. Find your loved ones, and ask them for support in these moments.

Asking for help when you need to rest will make you a better person, parent, and mentor. Even asking your child, "Mommy/Daddy had a hard day, can you come give me a hug, and let me rest for a little? I am hurting a bit," may spark a breakthrough in your relationship with your children. You are still the main pillar of support in their eyes, but suddenly you have humanised yourself, you've touched their emotional core, and now they realise the gift they are, and the important role they play in your life – not just the other way around.

You will be amazed how most children react to an expression of honest vulnerability after a hard day for you. Most will gaze with eyes of love and support, asking how to help make Mom/Dad feel better. Empower them to play that role; don't hide real adult emotions from them so that they stumble into them at age 18. Let them see the real you – they will love you even more for it. Just remember to express your emotions in terms a child understands. They may not be able to fully grasp a more sophisticated articulation. Keep it simple, pure, and heartfelt during these moments.

While Stuart Scott meant the message in a literal, physical sense, it is absolutely applicable in a mental and spiritual sense as well. The "work until you drop" culture is false virtue.

Instead, push yourself until you begin to feel yourself fray at the edges. Then push 10% more. After that, it is time to rest! Someone you love will pick up the fight in the meantime.

To be resilient in the long run, you need to value longevity. So, embrace your biological needs! Eat well, rest well, and have fun moving during the day. Otherwise, you may falter when it really matters, not because you weren't tough enough, but because you didn't take good enough care of yourself while preparing for the big moment. When establishing a new and refreshed meditative approach, resiliency and self-care go hand-in-hand: you can't maximise one without the other.

Not All Rest Is Created Equal

When lying down to rest, strive to get the most out of your rejuvenating activity – whether it be meditation or something more specific to your life and personal interests. Good rest does *not* always involve doing nothing – it means actively engaging in the simple process of "chilling out." In other words, some activities are more restful and restorative than others! Some people just enjoy being in nature. Surfers claim that surfing in the ocean is meditative. Others say the same about a walk in the rainforest.

As an example, a two-hour nap *sounds* nice, but a 25-minute nap has actually been proven to be *more* effective in restoring your energy levels, unless you are severely sleep-deprived. If you are waking up during the night, causing disruptions in the goal of uninterrupted sleep, you may be harming your waking day by failing to fully sleep through the night. In fact, good sleep hygiene is one of the most underrated aspects of our health.

So, if you feel your fatigue during the day stems from such poor sleep quality, and it is beginning to take a toll on your performance and mental health, it is time to pick a day on the calendar within the next two weeks and take the day off. Call it a mental health day, because that is actually what the focus is: restoring your mental and physical health. Start by getting a full-night's rest, and then plan to build your day around an activity or hobby that you absolutely adore. Enjoy the entire day, and accept no interruptions (except emergencies).

On your mental health day, you are aiming to uncover the kid at heart ... to rediscover what it is that makes you genuinely enthusiastic. That is what you will engage in all day. You won't be able to get that level of uninterrupted play when you return back to work, but make time for a mini version of that activity every day after. It will keep that day of fun with you, a reminder of what can make intense work so fulfilling: the joyful release of energy after a worthy challenge.

Conclusion

To finish up the discussion on resiliency, walk away with a simple goal in mind: hold onto the little silver linings and glimmers of good that pop up in your day. They are there if you look and listen close enough. It could be as small as someone smiling and waving to you while you walk the street. Maybe you look inside your fridge and realise how fortunate you are to have it stocked up. Maybe you read a good news story about a war hero going back to get their high school, university or college degree/diploma. Maybe you watch a YouTube video of a stray animal, on the brink of death, becoming a beloved household pet. Maybe you make a baby smile and giggle.

It is important to acknowledge the scale of tragedies we witness in our lifetime. It reminds us how cruel and vindictive the world can be, making it hard to find a quiet place mentally to meditate. However, it cannot be an excuse to ignore the rays of hope that shine through those moments – no matter how small or seemingly insignificant. Holding onto these precious, fleeting moments of joy are what will get you through the darkest nights and onto better days.

As long as you have breath in your body, there is still a chance for redemption. Until then, stay resilient. For blessed is the man who has suffered and found life.

Chapter 3

How to Access a Creative, Relaxed, Inquisitive Mindset: Genuine Awe

We live on an island surrounded by a sea of ignorance. As our island of knowledge grows, so does the shore of our ignorance.
– John Archibald Wheeler

There's a reason kids go from asking 400 questions a day at 4, to 50 a day at age 12. They've likely felt the sting of feeling "stupid" or "annoying" when asking a question that an adult or other child scoffed at. Because the world is so big and unknown to kids, they begin to act like "know-it-all" as a defence mechanism. It helps compensate for the quiet revelation they experience, in reality, not knowing much at all. As adults, we continue to act in the same way.

Instead of asking questions full of fascination and awe, adults and children begin just keeping questions to themselves. We pick up from others around that, "If the question's answer doesn't lead to you making money, or if it's not directly related to the current situation, then don't ask at all. Ignore it, get in a rush, and brush past whatever you don't know so you don't have to feel any fear of the unknown." At some point, most children decide they'd rather not ask questions at all, because adults stop engaging with them on a level of genuine awe – as if "growing up" means you need to act like you understand everything you need to know.

This chapter makes a powerful case for dispelling these myths of "ignoring what you don't know," and provides you with the tools to invoke a true, genuine sense of awe in ourselves and our children. When observing new phenomena or having a novel experience – both of which naturally happen to kids at a rapid rate, they love having an adult guide them along the way. Train ourselves and our children to get excited when we say, "I don't know," and help us all to maintain a wide-eyed enthusiasm for engaging with the frontier of new knowledge.

Before we get further into the biological, cosmological, and socio-historical case for awe, we first need to define a few key terms – awe and novelty. I'll discuss why these sensations are so vital to nurture in yourself and the kids you raise. I'll also discuss the frontier paradox regarding knowledge and ignorance, and provide tools to help you—and your children—grasp the remarkable scale of the world around you. To do so, I'll provide relative comparisons on how BIG the universe gets, and how SMALL the microscopic world really is, along with a discussion on why analogies can help us "map out the meaning" of a previously unfamiliar topic.

Revelations of the Unknown

Before we get into the rest of that, here's a story that illustrates how we can experience an overwhelming sense of awe. So much so, that we will question the very fabric of the world around us. Ernest Rutherford became known as the father of nuclear physics after running his famous "gold foil" experiment. In this test, the New Zealand scientist shot particles through a thin sheet of gold: only .00004 cm. He was stunned by the results: 99% of them went directly through the foil without any obstruction.

The discovery became a revelation for nuclear physics, as it implied that atoms, relatively speaking, have vast amounts of empty space between them. Rutherford had proven that 99% of the physical world was a void dotted with electron clouds and little nuclei. To put that in perspective, if the nucleus of an atom was the size of a baseball, electrons would be found as far as 2 miles away – everything in between would be static nothingness.

Needless to say, when Rutherford uncovered the phenomena, he was almost frightened by its implications. He was quoted as saying, "It was quite simply the most incredible event that has ever happened to me in my life. It was almost as incredible as if you fired a 15 inch shell at a piece of tissue paper, and it came back and hit you." As legend goes, Rutherford was afraid to get out of bed in the morning, for fear he'd fall through his floorboards. Being the only person on Earth who knew the true nature of the atomic world, it seemed so surreal that he had to pause and think, "Wait, now that I know this fact about the atomic world... am I going to fall into the centre of the planet?"

Ignoring the fact that, for some reason, Rutherford considered the particles in his bed more solid than the atoms comprising his wooden floor (sounds like an excuse to be lazy), the story vividly captures how even a fully-grown adult, jaded and unimpressed with the world around them, can suddenly be shocked into a state of a complete, transformational, metamorphic awe.

Here, Rutherford had expanded his own—and humanity's—frontier of knowledge. He had pushed our boundary of understand forward, enabling the breakthroughs in atomic physics that spurred the creation of nuclear power points, and, unfortunately, bombs. Regardless, much of the quantum world would have gone undiscovered for much longer had Rutherford not made his breakthrough discovery.

That is why we, as people, admire the scientists who innovate cutting-edge inventions, and love artists who stand on the border between "order" and "chaos." It's why we are enamoured with explorers or astronauts, who wander into the unknown from their comfortable perch within the known world. These endeavours usually come with a heightened sense of danger; they are perilous. However, the discoveries and revelations that occur on this border between "knowledge" and "ignorance" are profound in their life-changing implications. They lead a life exploring the frontier, where our "known" world bumps up against all that unknown. It is captivating to imagine these individuals giving shape, and making sense of, something humans previously had no conception of.

Just like Rutherford, or just like hearing your favourite artist for the first time, what we find on the frontier of the known world – the precipice where "known" meets "unknown" change our perception of reality, and how we can live within it. The "frontier" of our knowledge powers the drive for exploration, and simultaneously the desire for comfort within our own bubble of safety. It is within this space that pioneers turn abstract "nothingness" – something humans have no grasp of – into something concrete we can picture, observe, and discuss in the pursuit of greater knowledge/wisdom.

See the figure below for an illustration of your "area of knowledge" and the frontier paradox. While examining it, imagine that your "Area" of knowledge is a perfect circle. As your knowledge grows, let's say, just for the sake of simplicity, that "area" grows from 100 to 10,000 cm^2. That would mean your "radius for your circle of knowledge" also grew substantially!

Here's the rub—that also means your perimeter—your frontier of ignorance—grew alongside your growing area of knowledge. This is why people say things like, "The more you know, the more you don't know." As you grow your area of knowledge, you simultaneously become aware of all the layers of knowledge and intricacies of life you simply have no explanation for. The quote at the beginning of this chapter puts it well:

We live on an island surrounded by a sea of ignorance. As our island of knowledge grows, so does the shore of our ignorance.

– John Archibald Wheeler

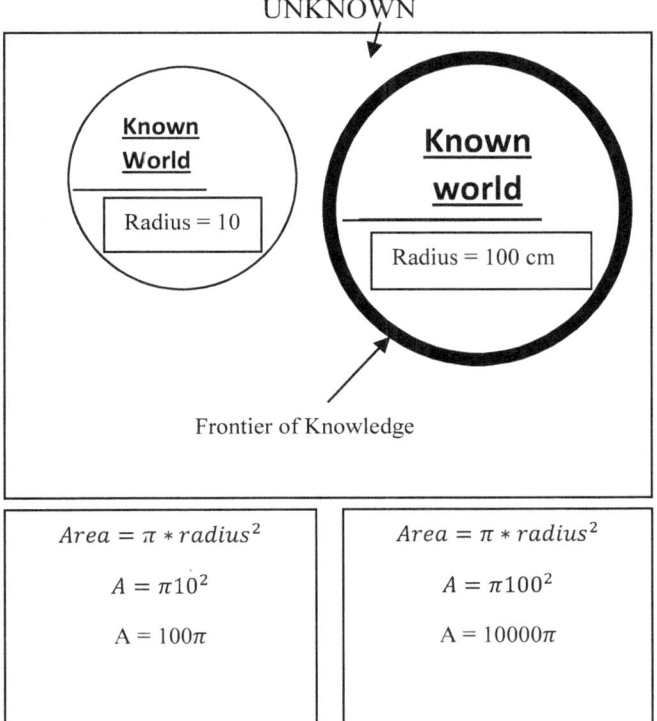

Known World

Radius = 10

Known world

Radius = 100 cm

Frontier of Knowledge

$Area = \pi * radius^2$

$A = \pi 10^2$

A = 100π

Perimeter (Circumference)
$= \pi * 2(radius)$

Perimeter = 20π

$Area = \pi * radius^2$

$A = \pi 100^2$

A = 10000π

Perimeter (Circumference)
$= \pi * 2(radius)$

Perimeter = 200π

I will refer to this phenomena as the "frontier paradox" – as knowledge increases, so too does awareness of our ignorance. The frontier, then, represents that notion that we are pushing our boundaries of knowledge, comprehension, and comfort. We are on the edge of order and chaos—and it's a fine line—like a razor. We can retreat back to the area we feel we can grasp and make sense of, but there is some mystery that lies beyond the frontier that humans want to explore and figure out.

In other words, the frontier of our knowledge—the line demarcating comfort and paint—wisdom and ignorance—the known and the unknown—is a powerful psychological concept. It is the line between the ordered world we understand and the chaos that envelops unpredictable surroundings. The place where there are no patterns you recognise, no similar structures, and no grasp of what anything signifies or represents. As we discuss psychological phenomena like "awe" and "novelty," as well as the scale of these events, it is important to remember the "frontier paradox." By expanding your knowledge, and learning all that falls within that area, the perimeter outside it expands. In other words, the more you know, the more you realise you don't know.

An ancient echo of this sentiment reverberates from ancient Grecians considering Socrates the "wisest man" in the city – for claiming he "knew nothing." By being aware of your area of knowledge and the frontier of your ignorance, you provide yourself—and your children—a proper conceptual framework to deal with pain and unknown mysteries within the universe.

The frontier paradox is, in some ways, a sister theory to the Dunning Kruger effect – a psychological phenomenon where incompetent or unknowledgeable people vastly overestimate their cognitive abilities in a given field. This is a similar idea: the less you know, the more you think you know because your perimeter of ignorance is small, protecting you from the true vastness of the unknown. So, ignorance may be bliss... but only temporarily. That is why discovering a new fact can be as scary as it is sublime – it reveals to you your capacity to push your frontier of knowledge while simultaneously reminding you how the universe can operate in such a profound, mysterious, seemingly esoteric way.

Tell your kid "I don't know," to inspire in them the sense to explore beyond the frontier. There is a solution, and that answer will manifest. However, maybe you just don't know how to answer it. Their life can involve answering those questions with you, and suddenly, you have a companion along for the ride: your kids!

When raising or teaching kids, one of the joys of the process is witnessing these moments of discovery happen at such a blistering pace. There are days where your kids have "a-ha!" moments that excite them, and make their minds ignite!

So, what happens when you discover something you don't know?

Defining awe vs novelty

The sensation of awe—the sublime—is as much a metaphysical topic as it is psychological. Awe is the experience, where something is so overwhelming in its emotional significance or profundity, that you feel a flood of sensations all at once. Some people may yelp in amazement. Others may begin crying. Some may simply get goosebumps and wide eyes, where the hair stands at attention on the back of your neck. The chills. Awe can induce an almost spiritual or religious experience. Seeing men on the moon for the first time invoked such a sense of awe that most people alive during that time remember exactly where and when they were when first hearing the news. The first-time people see an extraordinary formation in nature—like the majesty of the Grand Canyon—awakens a similar sentiment of bliss.

While there are many definitions of "awe" depending on the specific context, most awe-inducing moments spark powerful feelings of fear, vulnerability, admiration, mystery, vitality, oneness, freedom, and harmony—all at the same time. To sum up a sense of awe, it's the things in life that make you sit back, put your hands up, and say, "Woah" with eyes wide open. Even witnessing the fluttering wings of a hummingbird, or the beautiful path a butterfly takes riding the wind, can make you pause in a brief state of awe. An eye trained in awe recognises the simple serenity in these moments. Next time your child exclaims, "LOOK, a butterfly!" or, "Look, look, a birdie!" Look up and offer a gentle smile. They're right! It is remarkable, even if fleeting.

Recognising awe-inducing phenomena is crucial to your own self-realisation, as well as inspiring epiphanies in kids. It is often a memorable moment of pure "awe" that sticks with young people as they pursue their profession and passions. Maybe they're wowed by their favourite guitarist, and take up music as a result. Maybe they go with you to the hospital, and a doctor takes them on a tour of the facility, encouraging them to care for others, as well. Perhaps an archaeologist on YouTube relays the history of dinosaurs or the glory days of past civilisations, and all your kid wants to do after is dig and dig for the anthropological discovery of the century. You likely had moments yourself as a child, where an adult's performance wowed you to the point of being disoriented by such intense emotion and awe. There was life before, and what you thought you knew, and then there is what you see now.

Awe has been studied within medical contexts and proven to be extremely beneficial for well-being. It improves a connection to the sublime, and helps us feel humble, fulfilled, and motivated to further explore our frontier of knowledge. Affirming a child's moment of awe will help crystallise a deep, memorable bond that can last a lifetime.

Moments of awe become etched in our minds with vivid detail—especially when they have the added element of novelty. Novelty are experiences or events that "stick out" due to their unusual nature or wholly original presentation. When we encounter an external stimulus that bucks the patterned trend our brain is used to seeing, it lights up and registers, "Wait a minute! This is different!" On an evolutionary level, it does so in part to protect you, and ensure this novel experience is not a threat to your survival or health.

Beyond these conditions, seeking novelty is a sign of intelligence, openness, and greater divergent thinking. In other words, true novelty catalyses a burst of creativity in people, broadening their perspective and bringing joy from the charming originality and subversion of jaded/cynical/tired expectations.

A simple example of novelty-seeking would be travelling and tourism. You are breaking the pattern of what you normally see and do in your daily routine, making a fun novel experience. A more complex novel experience may be reading about a new idea or, even ingesting a psychedelic drug. That would like be a novel experience full of awe! And we're only half-joking – many adults rank an experience with a psychedelic as one of the most profound, meaningful experiences of their life. It's right alongside the day they got married, had kids, and events related importance. That's the power of a novel experience: it has the potential to be one of the most personally significant moments of your life.

To make the distinction clear, awe and novelty are not one and the same. You can see a beautiful sunset over the ocean every night, and if you have your head on straight, there is likely at least one second of "awe" that makes you feel amazing, humble, and small-yet-large at the same time. Small, because it's just little old you soaking in right where the sky and waves meet, but large because you are, in some way, a part of the vastness of this world. However, after seeing hundreds of sunsets, the "novelty" factor would likely wear off.

Now, let's say one night, you see the waves light up with electric blue hues due to bioluminescent creatures who are flooding the shore. Suddenly the same waves you've seen every night are lighting up in neon blue, like they're attending the world's largest electronic music festival. The bioluminescence would be a novelty factor added to the "awe" of a beachside sunset.

Training yourself, in a sense, to recognise when the elements of the world around you have come together in a powerful, harmonious way, in which you and people around you are the primary beneficiaries. By recognising awe and novelty on a grander scale, and registering the phenomena of it, you are more likely to recognise the same sensation when it appears on the scale of your personal life. These are the sentiments expressed in general clichés like, "It's all here for you," or "When you want something, the universe conspires to achieve it." The idea underlaying these common sayings are that, in a sense, for us to be here at this moment in time, there is undoubtedly a grand-scale miracle occurring at the quantum and cosmological level. However, because of the monotony of day-to-day life, it can be difficult to access this state of awe unless you have an ontological framework to remind you of its significance. The following sections will help you better understand the case of "awe" on a biological, cosmological, and socio-cultural level. That way, you will be well-equipped to recognise and appreciate moments providing a surge of novelty, refreshing your mind to the possibilities of higher-level activity in your own life.

Scaling "Awe"

If you were to tell your child that one million Earths can fit inside the Sun, they might retort, "Yeah well this one kid at school is already as tall as the teachers, so whatever." They don't know how big the world is yet, so they have no conceivable way to understand the scale of what you just told them! If you tell them that 1,000 metres are in one kilometre... does that really mean anything to a child in primary school? Maybe if you walked with them exactly that distance, and marked it, exclaiming, "We just walked exactly one kilometre, which is 1000x bigger than a metre," they may start developing a proper frame of reference for units of size and distance.

However, for more significant phenomena in the world around them—the kind that inspires sublime transcendence and fear of the unknown simultaneously—you yourself must have the proper conceptual scale to meaningfully relay the information. This section will reveal to you just how small, and big, the universe gets. It truly boggles the mind, and for our human brains, the vastness of space and the quantum nature of particles is virtually impossible to accurately picture. Even scientists who devote their entire lives to it do not really comprehend the scale of the phenomena they study– like the number of stars in the universe (200 billion trillion), or the number of atoms in a single breath of air (1 billion trillion). They simply do their best to make approximations and relative comparisons, while utilising helpful analogies that put the macro and micro world in terms humans can actually make sense of. Without properly comprehending the smallness—and vastness—of the phenomena we encounter in our lives, the significance of awe-inducing moments may go right over your head! Lack wisdom and miss out – like being the guy who laughs too late at a joke or misses the punchline completely.

First, we need to define macro—large scale—as any unit measuring larger than you—a single person. A mountain? Macroscale. A planet? Macroscale. 100,000 people dancing at a festival? Macroscale.

As we scale up in size exponentially, it gets difficult to conceptualise anything that is over 10^6 – or 1 million units in magnitude. To test this out, try picturing what two people look like standing next to each other, then 20, then 200, then 20,000, then 200,000, then 2,000,000, then 2,000,000,000... Notice how something happens there, between 200,000 and 2,000,000? By the time we're at 2 billion people, it's a totally abstract picture.

Picturing 2 billion people standing side-by-side each other with any clarity is simply impossible. It feels like the brain doesn't have enough bandwidth or film to picture

2,000,000,000 humans at once. The image in your head becomes so low-resolution that the difference between 2 million people vs. 2 billion becomes meaningless. Picturing 20 vs. 200 is a manageable task, but humans are not biologically equipped to accurately conceptualise orders of magnitude in the millions, billions, or trillions. Homo sapiens are built for comparisons, not counting. In fact, some tribal languages only have words to distinguish "small amount" from "large amount." The need to calculate the number of stars in the sky, or the number of atoms in your body, with precision was ultimately unnecessary for survival. However, for thriving, and achieving a meaningful understanding of the world in the 21st century, learning to frame the scale of awe-inducing phenomena is crucial. How can you raise kids to appreciate the enormity of the world around them if you cannot picture it yourself?

Without the proper conceptual framework, big numbers are virtually meaningless to us – even if they provide profound insight when understood in the correct scale. To drive the point home, consider that 1 million seconds is only 12 days, whereas 1 billion seconds is roughly 32 years… the magnitude of going from "millions" to "billions" sends our minds into a tailspin! Want to know how big numbers get? A googol (no, not the search engine), is 10 with 100 zeros. Easier enough to picture.

100000000 0000000 00000 0000000000 0000000000 00000 00000 0000000000 0000000000 000000 0000 0000 000000 000000 0000.

Here's the mind-boggling part: a "googolplex" is 10 with a "googol" zeros. We can't write that one down, because, and this is true, there isn't enough space in the entire universe to write out all the zeros in a googolplex. It is impossible to write out in numerical form in the physical world. If you filled every sheet of paper in the world with 0's you would not even begin to come close to the number of zeros in a googolplex. Tell that to your kid, and watch their head spin along with yours. They might end up being scared of math for a week.

To grasp how profoundly tiny some objects in the world get, it's important to give form to the "micro" scale – knowing how small a cell or an atom is in the scheme of things. Astrophysicist Neil De Grasse Tyson, in order to highlight the truly miniscule size of a molecule, relayed that there are more molecules in a single glass of water... than there are glasses of water you could scoop from all the world's oceans. One glass of water has over 1 septillion molecules of water, which is five orders of magnitude greater than 1 billion. If you converted all the water on the planet into water bottles, you wouldn't even come close to 1 septillion. That is how profoundly small a molecule of water is. You think the head of a pin is tiny? 5 trillion hydrogen atoms could sit on that pinhead. 5 trillion. Are you sure you have the conceptual scale to picture the bigness and smallness of the universe? Next time you look at the head of a thumbtack or nail around the house, think that a few trillion atoms may be floating above it – hopefully that induces a state of awe. When you breathe out, scoffing at the magnitude of that fact, remember that you just exhaled over 1 quintillion oxygen atoms: that's 1 with 18 zeros! Now, you can measure these things in the world—the micro and macro—but the implications for our perception of life are in some ways immeasurable.

Essential Analogies

Still, even knowing how vast—and tiny—our world can get is not enough to make sense of why these facts should invoke a sense of awe when we consider them. For that, we use analogies. Analogies help us map our understanding of one topic onto another through a relative comparison.

By making sense of the "unfamiliar" through metaphor, we can visualise in concrete terms a phenomenon that would otherwise be completely abstract. Tell a kid, "Life is like ice cream, enjoy it before it melts," and they'll begin to catch on to how finite time can feel.

To highlight how analogies can help us capture the scale and significance of a new topic, consider this famous analogy used in the show Cosmos, popularised by Carl Sagan. The "cosmic calendar" analogy scales all 13.8 billion years of the universe to a single calendar year. On the "cosmic calendar," all of recorded human history—from the Ice Age to the 21st century—occurs on the very last second of the very last day. Suddenly, the universe being 13.8 billion years old starts to make a lot more sense, and you have the conceptual framework to grasp the implication of humanity's place in the universe.

Why do analogies like the "cosmic calendar" help? Because humans don't have the conceptual understanding of what it feels like to live 1,000 years, let alone 13.8 billion. But 365 days? We can work with that. If you are trying to relate something of significance to your kids, look up or think of an analogy that puts it into concrete terms that they understand. They can map that understanding onto the topic you are discussing.

Keeping with cosmic theme, consider another analogy: the effect planets have on the fabric of space-time is like the effect dropping a bowling ball has on a trampoline. The fabric of the trampoline will indent where the bowling ball is, creating a literal curvature in the surface. That curvature is exactly how items with large mass—like planets—affect the fabric of space-time. Their gravity literally bends the fabric of space! Compare that to if you place a pebble a trampoline. There may be a slight dimple on the trampoline surface, but the effect is nothing like the bowling ball. That's why we don't have the gravity to bend space-time the way a planet does. In this analogy, we're the pebble!

To give a broader analogy on teaching or parenting, consider that teachers are like "ferrymen," helping their students cross the river of time. You help them on the boat, navigate choppy waters, and drop them off on the other side of the shore. At that point, they are ready to take care of themselves, and continue onto the next leg of their journey. However, they would never have gotten there without the ferryman! Ferrymen help people navigate dangerous rivers, teachers help navigate difficult times in life – the analogy fits like a glove.

Before continuing, take a word of caution on analogies! If they are incorrect, incomplete, or reduce the concept to an extreme, they end up damaging your conceptual understanding of the topic. For example, comparing the human brain to a computer strips away too much of our biology, rendering it an unhelpful comparison. We cannot perform raw calculations like a computer, and a computer cannot replicate the dynamic decision-making process the human brain utilises for even basic motor activities. That is why no self-driving cars have been released yet. The computer tech and software cannot replicate how we see and react. So, the analogy that the "human brain is like a computer," while sounding nice, is actually harmful to the conceptual framework of the brain and consciousness.

Avoid analogies that reduce or simplify a layered, detail concept into a broad, sweeping comparison. Instead, look for analogies that only try to explain one detail of the broader concept, rather than the entire concept itself. For example, it may help to say that part of the human brain can perform computations like a computer. However, you would want to avoid generalising the entire brain as just a biological computer, and vice-versa.

How Invoking Awe Translates to Living "The Good Life"

Look to invoke a genuine sense of awe, at least a few times a week. Stop and acknowledge some phenomena that makes you say to yourself, "Woah. I gotta figure out what's out there". Encourage your kids to do so, too. It speaks to a deep sense of discovery and pushes their frontier of knowledge.

Being able to recognise and respond to awe—even in seemingly mundane moments—stirs up a sense of excitement. It reminds us even on ordinary days, the sublime is there – there is majesty hiding somewhere. It is your job to seek and find it.

Doing so, as mentioned above also helps keep the ego in check, ensuring you don't fool yourself into thinking you, "Have it all figured out." Think about "know-it-alls" blathering on the internet about how right they are about every little thing: this is a serious example of the Dunning-Kruger effect! Regarding some of the remarkable phenomena we have discussed here, no one—not even the smartest minds on the planet—have a full explanation for their existence.

Most importantly, that spirit of awe will translate into other important areas of your life! For a quick example, consider the case of Apple founder Steve Jobs, who was inspired to give Apple products their defining "sleek, polished, beautiful" design aesthetic from an unlikely source... a college calligraphy class.

In his commencement speech at Harvard's 2005 graduation, Jobs remarked that he took the calligraphy class at Reed College, for no reason other than curiosity in design. He recalled how its nuance and melding of history, art, and design was "subtle in a way that science can't capture." 10 years later, when designing the first MacBook, all the lessons from that calligraphy came back to him. His awe and fascination with a seemingly unrelated topic—calligraphy— became the reason for Apple's emphasis on beautiful design and a delightful user interface.

Jobs could have easily said, "Pfft, I am going to make a personal computer and revolutionise the world. This handwriting stuff is bullshit. Who cares? I have software to write." No one would have blamed him. But, lacking the awareness to recognise the novelty and beauty of calligraphy would have meant Apple may have never become known for such well-designed, beautiful products. Just because a certain phenomenon or discovery does not directly link to your professional job or daily routine does not mean it isn't worth your time to think about and marvel at. Again – a genuine sense of awe invoked in one area can catalyse a breakthrough in one directly affecting your day-to-day life. Maybe you adjust your approach to your career that makes you both happier and wealthier. Maybe it plants the sapling of creativity, "out-of-the-box" thinking, and innovation in the minds of the kids you work with. Regardless, training yourself to recognise and acknowledge true novelty, and having a sense of awe about it, has the power to reframe your entire perspective on your—and your kids'—lives.

By having the awareness to recognise the awe calligraphy invoked in design, Jobs invoked a sense of fascination – a sense of awe – over how delightful he found the graphic design of calligraphy. The spirit of that fascination is why Apple, the largest company in the world, dominates the tech landscape with devices that users find not only powerful, but beautiful, and a true joy to use. Why did blackberry go the way of the fax machine, while Apple remains the preeminent leader in cell phones? Why do most people favour the iPhone over Androids? Because the iPhone is beautiful, sleek, and a joy to use. This design-centric ethos came from Jobs tapping into that sense of awe over what he learned in a calligraphy class. So, if you are trying to improve your own approach to business, or inspire the people you work with, pull inspiration from these unlikely places. When you do so, your true creativity will emerge, and your passion to create something great yourself—a novel innovation—will grow. At the very least, you will gain greater insight into living the "good life."

This is the power of out the box thinking to reveal insights we never previously considered – reaffirming our individuality and boosting our confidence to solve the challenges that arise in our life.

The Problem and Developmental Harm of Ignoring "Awe" and Novelty

Here's the danger in saying, "Meh" or "Who gives a fuck?" when discussing novelty and awe within the world around you. It risks making you small-minded and frustrated unable to imagine a solution to any problem. It also risks damaging your appreciation of the parts of your life you should be grateful for. For example, let's take the expansion rate/density of universe (or water molecule) example. If, in response the incredible scale and mind-blowing reality of these facts you shrug your shoulders and say, "I don't really give a shit, that means nothing to me," you may temporarily have a point. But with that reaction to novelty, you may not recognise the miracle of the fact you are breathing without major issue, have food stocked in your fridge, and (hopefully) a number of other seemingly "ordinary blessings" filling up your life. If you condition yourself to say to those 'ordinary miracles', "Yeah, who gives a shit; pretty much everyone has that stuff," you will enter a state of total disrepair and shock if the tides every turn. Your resilience will be damaged, and your perspective may be so distorted it won't recover in time.

You may have trouble sparking a sense of awe if you:

Don't know the question to ask?

Cannot meaningfully frame the true scale and implications of what is being discussed?

Ignore how expanding the frontier of your knowledge— or the depth of your comprehension—can refresh/ reinvigorate your perspective on your life—and the ways you can better it. From the microscopic to the cosmic level.

If you don't spark this sense of awe, it is easy to fall into to the trap of thinking, "Everything is boring, there is nothing for me to figure out or push my comprehension on further, and so I'm just gonna keep my head down." Furthermore, it will lead you to being very frustrated. When something inevitably goes over your head, and you have no good explanation for it, you'll feel anger, rage, and fear of the unknown rather than a compelling sense of excitement.

Worse, children crave a sense of novelty while learning more about the world – it's why they love stories of magic and grand tales of adventure on the frontier. If you, as their parent, begin acting and talking like you've already figured everything out, and they should stop asking questions, you develop uninspired, uninterested individuals. That's why kids stop asking questions by age 9-10; they are discouraged by the response of adults not encouraging them to explore or have a sense of wonder/awe about the world around them. Developing a 'wonder wall' where children can post their wonderings is a great way to encourage curiosity. These questions can be pondered over and researched as a family which develops closer bonds and sharing or the awe experiences. It is so interesting to learn the things that children are actually thinking about. In my experience it has never been about the English or Math lesson! Generally, it is about the world around us and human characteristics – give it a go for yourself!

Kids older than 8 can usually sniff you out invoking a false sense of awe, and it will make them roll their eyes. So, finding ways to spark a genuine sense of awe in yourself while relating to them will light up both you and your children, looking to explore what's on the frontier of your understanding/perceptions together. There is arguably no better bonding experience with your children than exploring the world with a genuine sense of awe, captivated by its novelty and seemingly inexplicable or incomprehensible phenomena. It boosts children's curiosity, confidence resiliency: curiosity to keep asking questions, confidence to pursue their dreams and aspirations, and resiliency to overcome the challenges that come their way.

Do you want your children to be physicists? Doctors? Famous painters or playwrights? Artisans and businesspeople of the highest order? Pursuing the career of their dreams? You must, and take this next line to heart:

Instil in your children a sense of awe when they observe the world around them and the novel phenomena they encounter every day. Remember, to a child, there are new experiences everyday—and arguably more often—because they simply know less. Their "frontier of ignorance" is smaller because their base of knowledge is smaller. You are there to guide these children to keep that genuine sense of awe towards the novel events they observe. In order to properly do that you must discover—or rediscover—that genuine sense of awe for yourself. Kids will take a cue from you on what to be awed by, especially if they feel the residue and resonance of you truly taking in the significance of the moment.

So, always remember the power and fascination of saying "I don't know." It reminds you there is something you can do to that further pushes your conception of the world—and of yourself—that increases your chance of truly living "the good life"—or even finally discovering what the "good life" is really all about. In order to do that, you must invoke a sense of novelty—a sense of awe. Don't forget the subatomic majesty going on, even in a simple glass of water. And never underestimate the vastness of the universe. Don't wait until you have a terminal illness to finally appreciate the beauty of a simple sunset. Many terminally ill patients remark they suddenly appreciate these simple moments of awe—but it wasn't the sunset that changed. The beauty was there all along. The beholder simply recognised the miracle within it. Nothingness is the norm in the vacuum of space. We are the exception. Chew on that wisdom for a bit when considering the biological, cosmological, and socio-historical cases for awe.

Medical Miracles – How Our Biology Organises Each Cell for a Unified Cause.

A quick disclaimer – I do not want this book to become justification for junk science or fraudulent claims that you can "pray away" cancer, or something of the sort. Giving people too much "hopium" in these instances could drive them to not seek medical treatment. Instead, these anecdotes are given to make clear that, alongside deploying the marvels of modern medicine, there are biological miracles that, arguably, have a basis in training the mind to organise its biology—each and every cell—for a unified purpose.

Take the case of spontaneous regression in cancer cells. It only happens in in 1 out of 100,000 patients… but that number is not zero. And even medical specialists cannot find an explanation other than calling it a miracle of our biology.

For a case study, let's look at a 74 year-old woman admitted to the St. James Hospital in Dublin, Ireland. Her worst fears were confirmed by a tissue biopsy test: she had squamous cell carcinoma. Cancer.

The doctors at first recommended amputation of the leg infected, but they questioned how a 74-year-old woman's quality of life would be impacted by such a drastic surgery. So, they decided to wait, agonizingly so, on what option of treatment best fit the tragic situation.

Then, something miraculous happened – the woman's skin cancer began just… Disappearing. Within 20 weeks she was completely cancer-free. No radiation. No chemo. No amputation. Of course, the old woman claimed it was the "hand of God," but a look closer medically speaks to a different potential: an organised anti-inflammatory response of the body.

Doctors don't know what unlocks the key to these rare cases, other than the immune response from the body somehow unifies to kill the cancerous cells. The fact there are phenomena where this does not happen gives us enough pause to realise there is something to visualising a quiet mind listening to every cell in its body. Even if it just inspires the individual to eat more cleanly and seek out immune-boosting treatments, cases of spontaneous regression prove the body's ability to beat back cancer by itself. While these only happen in rare circumstances at this point, it would take a truly unimaginative mind to not consider there may be a way to train the body's cells to organise this kind of immune response.

Channelling your body and minds focus toward exploring these miracles cannot be a *bad* thing. A miracle is not promised, but many would consider a late-stage cancer diagnosis a fatal diagnosis. Let this anecdote of spontaneous regression serve as an example of why there is a strong case to be made for having awe at the marvel of human biology. Despite its limitations and constraints, it appears there are ways for us to continue to inch past them. Even the fate of an individual with late-stage is not yet determined – there may be a solution hidden in your own biology.

So, embrace your biology, and be exactly who you are.

Mystery of DNA – the secrets encoded within our DNA.

The cosmic and quantum case for awe is easy to start off – did you know that, even with the highest-precision scientific instruments at our disposal, 95% of matter in the universe cannot be observed by humans? We only know it's there through mathematical calculation proving there must be *something* there that is forcing gravity to act the way it does throughout the universe. However, it cannot be seen, held, touched, heard, or tasted by people. None of our senses pick up on it.

95% of the fucking universe is totally out of sight for us. Look around you at all that is here. Can you believe that is only 5% of what exists? You may not be trying hard enough if you do not tap into a sense of awe of this fact! Even with all the advances in modern science and medicine, we've only tapped into 5% of the universe. There are events happening at the quantum scale we cannot see even with the most cutting-edge innovations in technology.

Here's another banger for you – some physicists argue that all matter is actually just a cornucopia of energy frequencies, waves, and *pure potential.* Put simply, all matter is just a body of vibrating energy coalesced together, and time does not exist. You are already dead, and you have not been born, and yet you are living, because all these moments stretch out over the universe.

If you need to drop acid to keep reading, we understand.

Because this book is meant to stir awe and not teach physics, I am going to take a metaphysical leap here, so stick with it. As you read, imagine how you communicate with others and express yourself. You'll notice certain phrasings in the vernacular may make sense on a deeply understood, yet rarely acknowledged level.

Think of yourself as a vibrating source of energy within the fabric of the universe, you can start to see how human consciousness and autonomy can play a role in our lives. You are the vessel, in a sense. To give it some artistic flair, we are electrons of the universe. We channel energy, and depending how you conduct yourself and orient your thoughts of being, you can emit the sort of frequency and vibration others pick up on. Like electrons in quantum theory, the potential is there – that part is up to you. There are potential outcomes that may be predetermined, but which outcome actually ends up happening on the moment examined is privy to your influence.

That's where phrases like "it's a vibe" come from – it is quite literally that! Or, when you here, "We're just on the same frequency," or "on the same wavelength." These are references to a deeply understood sense that human beings exert energy, and when those frequencies are listened to intently and balanced in harmony, miraculous outcomes can occur that were seemingly unpredictable or unimaginable just moments earlier.

It's that sense you can "feel" what's in the air around you. It's why attitude matters when approaching a situation or interaction. You can control yourself and align your being to bring out that light, and, in a metaphysical sense, seek that frequency and vibration being emitted from those around you.

To give a metaphysical justification for how this could happen at the macro level, consider the theory of quantum "entanglement." Quantum entanglement describes a phenomenon where particles are the quantum level, after directly interacting with each other, become "entangled" forever. In this context, "entangled" means they affect another's spin (their angle and momentum) at all times – even when unconnected. It speaks to an underlying fabric in the universe—some connecting energy—that permeates all space and matter.

No matter how far these two quantum particles get from each other, they continue to affect each other's spin state. Even if one billion light years apart!

This can only happen if everything is energetically connected on some level.

While we are not just quantum fields, it only takes a bit of an artistic leap of faith to see that maybe quantum entanglements happen between entire beings – for better or worse. If you have any loved one in your life who you always feel close and connected to, you guys likely connected on the quantum level the more people you find a positive connection with on that level, the more connected you are to the reality of our existence as a whole.

So, while everything is energy, these appearances matter! There is something beyond your sense and beyond your mind—the Self—but it does not help to get your head too much in the clouds! We all share these appearances, and they matter for contending with the challenges we face in the world every day. You are free to choose, only bounded by your own humanity, and the structures erected from before your time.

In fact, quantum theory has proven determinism false for this reason. The world is not that predictable or fatalistic, and neither are you. There is autonomy in how you get in touch with every fibre of your being, from the back of your head all the way to front, down to your tippy-toes, and back again.

That's why people say you are glowing or radiating—it's picking up on your light at a biological—and quantum—level!

When we say be your biology—be who you are—consider one final cosmic trait all humans share. To make the long story of the big bang short, there have been three major generations of stars. The first star generations held only helium and hydrogen, but when exploding as supernovas, heated together to form all the elements in the periodic table today. They all came from helium and hydrogen, exploded into gaseous space dust.

Therefore when we say to dust we shall return, it is stardust. We are stardust – our matter. Our being. You can think of humans as brutish, dumb, short-sighted, selfish, egotistical beings, but we are also the amalgamation of 13.8 billion years of creation. Those billions of stars, forming and exploding in brilliant light, those billions of years of gas and matter slowly pulling together into planets… in a sense, it was all done just for us to have a chance to walk around for a few decades.

You could argue we are the most refined creation of the universe with the most detailed systems that make us function. If there is a God, he may have gotten bored with inanimate stars, comets, and planets floating in the abyss of space. In a religious or spiritual sense, I see it as we were moulded from stardust for a simple reason: to make God less lonely. That's probably why religious folk like to feel "close to God." He appreciates the company. We are, as far as we know, the most intimate creation of the universe. Stars may be larger and grander, but nothing is more personable and unpredictable than humanity.

Let's do a quick mindset check – I hope you have a newfound appreciation for what enduring just beyond the point of "comfortability." You appreciate that being kind and positive are good traits and hopefully make up most of your day… but modern society tends to overvalue being "nice," to the point of "toxic positivity." We hope now you can appreciate the moments you feel down, doubtful, anxious, angry, or sad – the fact you can feel means there are ways you can rebuild your mental pathways for a better and brighter future. Mindfulness meditation—even 15 minutes a day—can have a transformative effect on your day-to-day approach at this point.

Beyond highlighting the trait of resiliency, make sure you are able to enter a genuine state of "awe" before reading the next section. Consider the miracle of your biology. The fact you are conscious at all, and the fact not every system in your body is going haywire (even if it feels like it temporarily), is a delicate miracle of the universe.

Chapter 4

Let's Have More Fun!

When I think about people who like to have fun, the first person that comes to mind is Sir Richard Brandson. Sir Richard has built his massive wealth and successful business on laughter and fun. There have been many failures along the way but he has always maintained that unless he is having fun it is not worth doing. He readily admits that there is definitely the requirement to work hard in his business but he ensures that his sense of fun is paramount to the soul of his company. Sir Richard, as the leader of his company says he leads by example. He is not the CEO sipping sherry on the corner with the other executives, he is leading the fun for his staff. Sir Richard appears to me to be someone living life to the fullest, taking risks, learning from his mistakes and being genuinely happy! His sense of fun has definitely paid dividends financially, however he is always quick to say he "never did it for the money!"

So why have we forgotten to have fun? I often say to teachers in my school, "If you are not having fun, the children in your class aren't!" Yet, this seems to be a very difficult point to get across. The response is generally, "we have so much curriculum to get through," "the kids take too long to complete work", "the behaviour of the children will get out of control if we have fun", "I won't be able to control my class!" Parents also place so much pressure on student grades and expect unrealistic workloads for children. There is a lot of research that indicates that homework in primary schools has little or no effect on children's academic performance, yet many parents complain that their children should be doing more and even enrol them in Saturday tutoring. Wouldn't families be happier if they went on a bush walk without their phones, spent time in nature and were present with each other? The children may not be so anxious and be able to relax and learn much easier when the time is right.

Children are our future, but our track record for improving the wellbeing of our children is not great! Our children communicate with us in various ways to get what they need. If these needs are not met it can significantly impact their chances for positive mental health throughout their lives. I think it is interesting that Dr Gabor Mate suggests that ADD can cease being an issue if the family dynamics changes. He does not discount medication but suggests that many mental health conditions of our children are the result of something going array in their most formative years. As parents, teachers, significant others and role models, we contribute to children's mental health by understanding the function of their behaviours specific to the period of life and by paying attention to their reactions to us and the world around them. We contribute to positive mental health in a child by allowing them to develop self-esteem, to feel secure, to develop good relationships with others and to evolve in an environment respectful of all human rights. We can teach our children the skills and strategies to support positive mental health at all stages of their lives. We can teach them to identify, understand and deal with their emotions.

It is estimated that 50% of adult mental illness begins before the age of 14. Depressive disorders and conduct disorders count for three of the five leading causes of mental health issues in children aged 5 to 14 years from the (Australian National Children's Mental Health and Wellbeing Strategy). There is evidence that poor mental health during childhood can lead to longer term mental health issues. This is why it is so important for us to look for solutions and strategies to support our children.

For over 20 years, I have been a school principal in many different school settings and overwhelmingly have noticed the increase in mental health issues with students getting younger and younger and more frequently. The majority of the mental health conditions that I come across in primary schools are things like anxiety and depression, eating disorders and ADHD. Sometimes it's difficult to tell the difference between feeling anxious about something that we don't want to do and actual anxiety disorders. Many parents want to take away any obstacles in the path of their children if they think that it might cause them to be anxious. This doesn't help them. Avoidance only makes the problem worse. We all need to do things that we don't want to do. It is important to talk to children about working through some of the difficult things. If we don't allow children to do anything difficult as young children then how can they ever get the skills when they get older? We need to teach them some techniques to deal with the anxiety rather than take away the event or experience.

There is always a place for negative feelings. We need to have them but we also need to learn how to deal with them and move on and replace them with positive feelings.

The child can, like the adult, experience temporary discomfort. In some cases, this state can last and become more intense. It can also evolve into a mental disorder. It's important to remember that many conditions can get better quickly if caught early enough.

When a malaise sets in a child, several aspects of his life can be disrupted: relationships with others, self-esteem, sleep, food, stress level, school results, involvement and motivation in daily activities.

Children are frequently anxious. It may be a transitory moment linked, for example, to school learning. A manifestation of anxiety in itself is not necessarily pathological. The adults around the child must ask themselves about the signs' importance and duration to assess whether help is needed. To assist the child to work through the issues. The best way to do this is to be present and listen to the concerns of the child and help them to face the fear and move forward.

In primary school, more children are presenting with "school refusal" which is worrying. This behaviour is one of the "silent" issues that can go unnoticed or not followed up by education professionals as children who are not there do not create problems in the classroom. However, these should alert us as much as more "noisy" problems. Good educators and parents should investigate the cause of the school refusal in the early stages so that plans can be developed to re-engage the child into education. Educators should continue to consider and adjust their teaching programs and teaching styles to engage children in their education, but that is a whole other book!

School gives all children access to a common base of knowledge: reading, writing, and counting. These acquisitions can be difficult for many reasons. I personally like the work of Guy Claxton who talks about "Learning powers," where dispositions such as curiosity, determination, imagination, collaboration and reflection are more highly valued than test scores. I have introduced these into my school where the engagement of children has increased, especially neuro-diverse children who can easily experience success. These "Superpowers" as I call them allow a child to both mobilise their reasoning skills and their curiosity. They accept not knowing, making mistakes and starting over.

If the difficulties persist, the child must be able to benefit from an assessment of his situation. They can be indicative of a malaise, be explained by possible "dys" disorders, such as dyslexia or dysgraphia, or attention deficit disorder with or without hyperactivity (ADHD), characterised by difficulty concentrating. At school, specific arrangements can help the child. Back to Sir Richard, he was diagnosed with dyslexia as a child, which made learning difficult for him. He was never a straight A student! He does however possess the "superpowers" of determination, imagination, curiosity, reflection and socialisation. Aren't these great attributes to acknowledge as most important for our children throughout their lives instead of having them define themselves by a grade or a number at the end of their schooling. I have found the for our neuro-diverse learners, praising their "Learning Superpowers" instead of their academic grades has in fact improved their academic performance and drastically improved their self-esteem, as suddenly school is a place they can succeed.

There are many individual programs in schools to try and address the notion of building resilience. These programs are ad hoc and reliant on teachers who are passionate about mental health. Most schools will have a whole school social emotional program or behaviour management program but very few schools will ensure that this is done consistently in every classroom. I believe that a social emotional program coupled with mindful meditation on a daily basis can help us tackle the problem of poor mental health. If we give children the skills to manage their thoughts and emotions early, this becomes a superpower that they can carry through their whole lives.

It is through play that children discover and understand the world around them. While having fun, they work on essential aspects of their development, including strengthening their motor, cognitive, social and emotional skills. However, the power of play goes beyond early learning: it plays a key role in the development of your child's mental health – and yours! Find out why taking the time to play is both fun and healthy.

As your child's first playmate, you can provide opportunities for them to learn and bond at home. Sharing moments of joy, relaxation and learning makes children and their caregivers feel closer. When you play together, you can see the world through their eyes. By providing your child with love, comfort and attention, you are laying the foundation for developing the emotional and social skills they need for their mental health and future well-being. Playing, dancing and singing are great ways to release stress for both you and your children. When you have a good time and laugh together, your body releases endorphins that promote a sense of well-being. Even short periods of play can help adults not lose sight of their ability to support their child. It gives you the opportunity to forget about your job and other commitments.

Long periods of stressful situations can affect a child's physical and mental health. Playful, positive and constructive relationships with adults can help minimise these effects. Research has also shown that spending time on playful activities even protects children from the negative effects of prolonged exposure to stress.

Children with complex emotional issues often use play as a means of expression. The game allows them to express things that they find difficult and for which they don't quite have the words yet. Giving children space to play allows them to process feelings like pain, fear or loss while still being able to behave like children. By inventing games to recreate painful moments over and over again, toddlers try to understand the effects of what happened. For example, if your child has witnessed an argument between two adults, they may want to recreate that conflict with their dolls.

There are studies that examine the health impact of damaging behaviours, including physical inactivity, smoking and medical noncompliance. Similar to this, emphasis is also laid to understand the impact of particular healthy behaviours like having a proper sleep routine, hygiene and eating a proper diet. On the other side, very little emphasis is given to the aspect of engaging in leisure or enjoyable activities and its implications on mental health that holds immense beneficial properties for us.

Enjoyable leisure activities are graded as pleasurable activities in which people engages voluntarily so that they remain free from work-related demands and other responsibilities. These activities can be your favourite sport, hobbies, socialising with other people or spending some time with nature. Why might these activities be beneficial? The fact is that enjoyable activities and relaxation time is beneficial, particularly during the time of stress and the post-stress recovery period. Vacations, coffee breaks, siestas and other leisure activities act as 'breathers' that offer a chance to take a break and engage in a pleasurable diversionary activity along with inducing positive emotions that reduce stress levels. You can also consider these enjoyable activities as 'restorers' that facilitate from stress recovery by replenishing damaged resources. Resultantly, indulging yourself in different leisure activities will bring in several healthy activities in the context of daily life.

Chapter 5

Opportunity to Disconnect

With our busy days and all the time we spend in front of the screens, going out for some fresh air allows us to take a break. Sitting at the foot of a tree or on a bench, and even while walking, we take the opportunity to breathe deeply, which we tend to forget to do in the daily grind.

Isn't nature a great place to put your cell phone aside? Beware of the trap of wanting to photograph everything, and especially the crazy time it has taken to get THE photo for social networks. Let's put our screen down more often to fully enjoy the present moment!

Let yourself be lulled by the song of birds or the sound of a stream, admire the different shades of green in the trees, put your hands in the ground while gardening, hug a tree (yes, yes!), walk barefoot in the grass, breathing in the smell of undergrowth or the scent of flowers are all ways to awaken our senses and marvel at nature.

We just have to slow down and be attentive to what surrounds us, regardless of the corner of nature in which we find ourselves. Let's enjoy it all year round because each season offers its share of unique experiences.

According to hundreds of medical studies, greener cities could decrease the prevalence of stress by around 39%, the prevalence of depression by 7%, the risk of diabetes by 14%, the risk of high blood pressure by 13%. And 10% to 20% premature general mortality.

As such, physicians have recently mobilised for urban greening in order to protect trees, wooded areas and natural environments and to promote massive tree planting. "Spending time in nature" will perhaps become the most popular medical prescription!

Although the experience of the COVID pandemic was horrific for many of us, it did force us to look at life very differently. During the lockdowns which were quite lengthy here in Australia, we were allowed to go outside for exercise for one hour a day. This was very difficult for many of us, but I remember walking along the beach during my one hour release and noticing many aspects of nature that I had not seen before. I had the experience of engaging more fully with the beauty around me. Maybe because it was less crowded, I didn't have to contend with the crowds at all, I was able to connect to the beauty around me.

My husband loves to surf, he says that as well as being at one with the ocean and in the present moment, he is alive in all five senses. When at work, one sense can dominate and there is always an element of stress (he too is a school principal). In the ocean he describes a "buffet of sensations" from which to select the experience. Once his feet hit the sand after a long surf, the feelings of wellbeing remain. During COVID we were not allowed to surf so it forced him to find his quiet place in other corners of nature. We had many experiences of birds sitting on our balcony that we had not noticed before and their songs all sounded different. We became so aware of these that we even began knowing which birds were present at any time by the sound of their songs.

The key is not to just be in nature but to connect with it. Next time you are out, notice the flowers and their individuality, their smell and the perfection of symmetry that they are. Focus your attention on the beauty around you, do this for a few minutes and increase this focus each time you go out, I guarantee that you will start to feel happier, that is mindfulness!

Chapter 6

The Dunedin Multidisciplinary Health and Development Study

The most recent studies from the Dunedin project have some really fascinating results. If we control our emotions, thoughts and behaviours, it leads to positive aging. Studies of self-control across the first 10 years of a child's life show that as adults, children with good self-control were better equipped to manage a range of later life health, financial and social demands. Children' s self-control can be separated from their social class origins and intelligence. Children were also able to shift naturally in their level of self-control across adult life. This ability to adjust suggests the possibility that self-control may be malleable and a target for interventions.

The Dunedin study found a pattern of reduced Neo cortical thickness appearing to be common across all forms of mental disorders and may represent a transdiagnostic feature of general psychopathology. The children in this study with low self-control were more likely as teenagers to smoke tobacco drop out of school become teen parents. It is well known that high family social class and good intelligence influence children's life success and this was also seen in the Dunedin project. Dunedin children with greatest self-control of significantly are more likely to be from socio-economically advantageous families. Children with greatest self-control also had significantly high IQ's. There is more interesting info in this study.

This experiment began in 1972 when doctors decided to study the future consequences of possible birth complications on children born at the Dunedin maternity ward. This is how, in 1975, researchers assessed the development of 1,037 3-year-old children, i.e., most of the children born in Dunedin (+90%) between April 1972 and March 1973. Following this assessment, it was decided to follow them throughout their lives. This study, carried out in stages over time, gave rise to multiple publications and a series of documentary films made in 2015 by Paul Casserly: "Who are we? The great experience".

This experience, therefore, seeks to "understand what makes us who we are". The scientists who initiated it have set up an ambitious methodology for this. First of all, the people followed are followed in the greatest confidentiality, whatever their situation. This would create a real confidence to express oneself freely.

The evaluations were done periodically between 3 years and 50 years. The last was therefore carried out in 2019, for the 45 years of the people followed and are ongoing.

At each stage of the study they participate in Dunedin in interviews, tests, medical examinations and surveys where they are evaluated on their health as well as on their personal and professional life. Currently 96% of people, alive, followed since birth are still participating in this study. This record follow-up rate in a longitudinal study would be due both to the framework of trust and interest created, but also to the financial and human resources mobilised for the study. The many people who no longer live there (2/3) have their travel and stay covered by the study wherever they are in the world. Researchers and investigators follow their migration to be able to stay in touch with them.

This unique study in the world has highlighted multiple elements. The most emblematic piece of information from this survey has put the debate between the innate and the acquired in humans back on the table. Indeed the study would show that the temperament of a 3 year old child would be generally the same in adulthood. Since such important and decisive elements for the future are played out at such a young age, scientists recommend focusing on public policies for early childhood to develop balanced pathways. Learning self-control from childhood would be the solution to build personal and professional success and better health.

The study also analyses the causes of juvenile delinquency, the impact of television on school results, lack of sleep on obesity and many other things. But the Dunedin study, like many studies, raises controversies and particularly when this research reveals that domestic violence would be due as much to the man as to the woman. The difference in impact would be on the different constitutions of the two sexes.

Despite controversies, this research has become a world reference. She would even have participated in the fight for the abolition of the death penalty for minors in the United States. So tomorrow, early childhood policy will become the top priority in political programs as well as in government actions.

Meditate as an early intervention

"To meditate is to become familiar with what is happening in the present moment inside and outside of oneself. We open our senses. We hear the noises, the sounds, the silence; we smell the smells; we see colours and shapes, and the effect is a calming of the mind," explains Nicole Bordeleau, author, meditation teacher and founder of the YogaMonde studio, on the south shore of Montreal.

There are several forms of meditation, says Ms Bordeleau: "You don't have to sit for hours in the lotus position like a Buddhist monk to meditate. Most types of meditation taught today have no connection to religious or spiritual movements."

Meditation can, by reducing our stress levels, have a beneficial effect on our physical health. One of its benefits is to reduce the risk of stress-related diseases.

Researchers and medical doctors have shed light on the effects of stress on the body. A number of illnesses are directly related to stress. This is the reason why doctors recommend the practice of meditation to their patients in order to reduce their level of stress. The practice of meditation is recommended, because it has the effect of slowing down our heart rate and lowering our blood pressure. Meditation is even recommended to strengthen our body's immune defences. Hospitals and clinics go so far as to offer meditation courses to their patients.

Following on from the results of the Dunedin project, It makes sense then that we would teach our children to find their still, quiet place within and start to teach them how to meditate. Giving children experiences and opportunities to connect to nature regularly and modelling for them our own connections is a good start. It would be a valuable strategy to be able to call upon during the inevitable stresses of our lives.

Psychological benefits

According to Ms Bordeleau, meditating can strengthen our memory, reduce our mental fatigue and improve the quality of our sleep. "Studies have also shown that the regular practice of meditation helps to live better with stress, reduce anxiety and better manage our emotions, adds Laurence De Mondehare, doctoral student in psychology and research assistant for the Research Group and Intervention on Mindful Presence (GRIPA) at UQAM. Meditation can also improve our attention span, concentration and mood. It helps to develop a certain clarity of mind and compassion for ourselves and others."

Meditation leads to a deep state of relaxation and a calm mind bringing us mental benefits. Studies have shown meditation's positive effect on the brain and improving memory. In addition, its practice increases our ability to concentrate and pay attention. Meditation can allow us to increase our ability to concentrate in areas as diverse and varied as those relating to sport, education, the world of work or leisure. When we are focused, we become more efficient and productive. Great sports personalities as well as great champions have indicated that meditation has allowed them to increase their ability to concentrate, thus enabling them to reach the heights of their discipline.

Emotional benefits

Your emotional well-being can also be improved through meditation. It brings you inner peace and joy. Through meditation, you can reduce anxiety and depression caused by loneliness and disappointments in life. When these are the consequence of emotions such as feelings of isolation or loneliness we experience a feeling of isolation and loneliness or sadness due to the loss of a loved one in life, meditation can be a complement the support we receive from professionals.

When we meditate, we enter a place of happiness and peace within ourselves. We become more positive. We realise that beyond our daily problems that are the cause of our emotional pain, there is a source of joy inside of us that we can step into and feel more joyful. Meditation helps us recharge, invigorate and regenerate.

When we are happier, we are calmer and more balanced. This will create a ripple effect that will radiate to others. Meditation can improve our relationships with family members, friends, spouse, co-workers, and even our neighbourhood and community.

Physical benefits

Because meditation reduces our stress response, it has beneficial effects on heart health, by lowering blood pressure and slowing heart rate. "Meditation can also remedy various small everyday problems," says Nicole Bordeleau. It can relieve digestive issues, release tension in the shoulders and neck, and reduce migraines, joint pain, and back pain. In

North America, some 240 pain clinics use meditation to help patients manage chronic pain. If it does not cure it, meditation makes it easier to live with it, often because it calms the strong emotions that accompany it.

Studies have also shown that meditating improves the quality of life of patients. Thus, a clinical trial, led by researchers from the University of Montreal and the CHU Sainte-Justine, revealed that mindfulness meditation can improve mood and sleep in adolescents with cancer.

"Meditation is not a magic pill that erases all ills," warns Nicole Bordeleau. "But it is an extraordinary tool to improve our quality of life. For a very long time, we took care of our bodies; the next decade will be that of the mind," she concludes.

The first successful scientific studies on meditation and the brain only date back to the 2000s, with the appearance of brain imaging technologies. They are carried out in the United States by two pioneers: Francisco Varela, a French neuroscientist of Chilean origin, and Richard Davidson, director of a neuroscience laboratory at the University of Wisconsin. Antoine Lutz, who had completed his thesis on consciousness with Francisco Varela, joined them in 2003. He was responsible for carrying out experiments on "expert" meditators, that is to say, those with at least 10,000 hours of practice – duration equivalent to the traditional Buddhist retreat of three years. Using imaging techniques, he compares the brain activity of expert and novice meditators. "We were the first to show that meditation causes functional changes in the brain," says Antoine Lutz. It induces a reorganisation of neuronal activity. This is called neuroplasticity, i.e. the ability of the brain to be modified—

including in its structure—by lived experience. It can be observed, for example, in a professional pianist or a London taxi driver: the cerebral region which controls the movement of the fingers for the first or the memorisation of the streets for the second is more developed than in an ordinary subject. "We can train certain regions of our brain as we do exercises to develop our muscles," assures Antoine Lutz. "The regular practice of meditation thus has a physiological effect on the brain: this translates into the activation of certain areas that control our attention, our emotions, our presence in the world and to others."

The researchers observed that a meditation session was made up of cycles consisting of four phases: first the wandering of thoughts, then an awareness of distraction, followed by the reorientation of attention and the return to concentration. Thanks to advances in brain imaging, they found that for each of these phases a specific brain network was activated. Experiments carried out at the laboratory of the University of Wisconsin have shown that in expert meditators, brain activity in areas related to attention was more intense. Other experiments were conducted in subjects before and after a three-month meditation retreat. *"We have shown that intensive meditation exercises help sustain attention and improve brain alertness,"* continues Antoine Lutz.

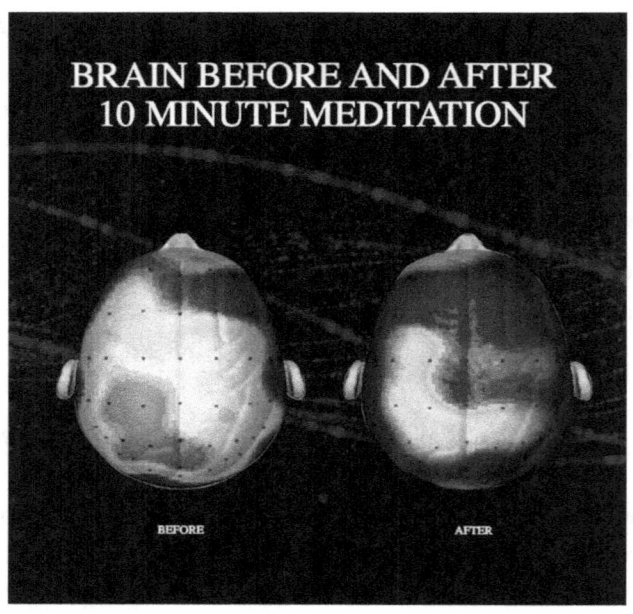

BRAIN BEFORE AND AFTER
10 MINUTE MEDITATION

BEFORE   AFTER

Vestergaard-Poulsen P, van Beek M, Skewes J, et al. Long-term meditation is associated with increased grey matter density in the brain stem. Neuroreport. 2009 Jan 28;20(2):170-4.

A 40% reduction in the risk of relapse after severe depression

This result opens promising clinical perspectives in the field of the treatment of chronic pain, but also in that of the treatment of depression. Meditation thus allows depressed patients to detach themselves from negative thoughts and rumination, which characterise this state. A Canadian team has shown that six months of mindfulness meditation practice (combined with cognitive therapy) after an episode of severe depression reduced the risk of relapse in depressive patients by 40%. Still other studies have focused on the practice of compassion, the most advanced form of Buddhist meditation. They revealed high amplitude oscillations in the electrical activity of the brain in a certain frequency band, a sign of significant synchronisation of neuronal activity between different areas of the brain. This phenomenon, which has not given up all its secrets, could explain the broadening of the field of consciousness in experienced meditators.

Meditation does not only act on the brain but on the whole body

As we have seen, meditation induces not only changes in the functions of the brain but also changes in its structure. Using magnetic resonance imaging (MRI), researchers have observed that brain tissue in the left prefrontal cortex—involved in processing attention, perception and internal bodily sensations—thickens in heavy exercisers, to the point of compensating in some for the loss of grey matter due to aging. Other studies, finally, suggest that meditation does not only act on the brain but on the whole body. It could thus reduce inflammatory phenomena and slow down cellular aging.

Despite its clinical effectiveness, the mechanisms of action of meditation are still poorly understood. Several laboratories around the world are trying to understand them. This is the subject of the ERC research project led by Antoine Lutz at the CRNL. It aims to study the processes that underlie the practice of mindfulness at the experiential, cognitive and neural levels. Meditation has not yet delivered all its secrets.

Joe Dispenza – Bringing mindfulness to everyone through guided meditation

I have also been working on the benefits of meditation presented by Dr Joe Dispenza, Doctor of chiropractic, author, researcher and successful American speaker, who devotes his work to developing methods of personal development that allow everyone to reach their full potential.

Made famous thanks to the docu-fiction *What do we really know about reality?* (What the Bleep Do We Know!) released in 2007, Joe Dispenza has quickly become one of the greatest mindfulness and personal development figures in the world.

Based on the search for mindfulness using meditation and exercises to improve the way you use your brain, it has already enabled thousands of people to live more fulfilled and even, quite simply, to change your life.

Self-healing and the placebo effect

The two main angles of his work are self-healing and the placebo effect. The latter is, according to him, proof that the power of the mind can have very real and physical repercussions. Thus, in his book, he mentions many documented cases where patients have succeeded in remedying various pathologies, such as depression, arthritis or heart disease, and this simply thanks to the power of this famous placebo effect.

To do this, he bases himself on the principle of neuronal plasticity (a term that describes the mechanisms by which the brain is capable of modifying itself) to imagine exercises that generate a lasting and in-depth change in the individual. As indicated by the title of his work *Breaking The Habit of Being Yourself* to create yourself again, the idea is to give birth to a new and better version of yourself that allows you to live better and improve different sectors, physical or psychological, of his own life.

Using Meditation to Heal the Mind...And the Body

Healing by the sole power of thought, such is his credo. No need to resort to drugs or surgery, personal development is within everyone's reach, provided they devote their energy to the desired changes.

Thus, neuronal plasticity makes it possible to act on the body, and not simply on the mind! Joe Dispenza experienced this: after being the victim of a car accident which resulted in fractured vertebrae, Dispenza refused the operation deemed necessary by the doctors in order to allow him to walk again. Instead, he decided to try to heal himself using his willpower, and only managed to walk again three months later.

This extraordinary experience gives full weight to Joe Dispenza's speech and is an impressive example of the power of the will and, therefore, of the brain. In order to obtain results, Dispenza recommends meditation as a practice for working on neuronal plasticity.

Rather than leaving those who wish to heal and change their lives through meditation on their own, Joe Dispenza uses guided meditation. In this mode of meditation, the listener is guided by a narrator who helps them stay focused and tells them what to think about and where to direct their attention. This allows you to reach a deep meditative state, a state necessary in order to use your brain and mind to the best of your ability to allow the desired changes to take place.

One of the specificities of Joe Dispenza's work is that he begins his guided meditation sessions with a section dedicated to the notion of space, acting as a prelude to meditation itself. The goal is to let yourself be guided in order to reach a physical and mental state that promotes calm and concentration. Thus, this prelude to guided meditation aims to leave the analytical state that separates the conscious mind from the subconscious mind.

Once this stage is reached, the body and mind are ready to experience what he calls elevated emotional states, fuelled by positive energy and able to communicate with our genes and the body's internal environment to let the changes operate. This allows you to bring about a change in your body using your mind.

Dr Joe Dispenza and his research team have been at the forefront of meditation research in the last few years. Recently, his researchers from University of California, San Diego have discovered that the body is capable of making its own chemicals for healing. Some interesting experiments have taken place on the blood of meditators, with the main focus on a multi-omic characterisation of the plasma in their blood. This means that meditation may have an effect on epigenetics which will have enormous implications for the future of healing. There will be more findings from this research published in the near future.

How can we help our children?

It was the work of Dr Joe Dispenza that inspired me to consider the impact that meditation might have on the mental health of our children. Upon returning to my job as a school principal, I became aware very quickly that there had been a definite increase in the numbers of children taking medications for mental health conditions. It was also concerning to me that many of our children required melatonin to assist them with sleeping. Why were our children so anxious and depressed? What was our schooling and home life situation doing to our children that they required medications to function?

Considering the research on mental health and the brain physiology, coupled with research on the impact of meditation versus medication, I decided to implement a meditation project at my school in collaboration with Bond University on the Gold Coast in Australia and Dr Joe Dispenza. Children were divided into two groups. 4.5-8 year old children and 9-12 year old children. Each class teacher would provide 3-5 minutes or 5-8 minutes depending on age, a guided meditation for their class each day. Once a week students would complete a survey to measure changes in their mental health over a ten week period.

The results of the study were fantastic! The results were statistically significant to show a decrease in emotional and behavioural difficulties over the time period as well as an increase in happiness and mindfulness. Younger children self-reported an improvement in their academic performance also. Internal school behaviour management data indicated a reversal of a three-year trend where behaviour incidents actually decreased over the ten week period where there had been an increase in the previous two years.

Anecdotally there were many observations by both myself and class teachers to indicate an overall improvement in mental health. Teachers reported that children seemed to create better relationships with each other as time progressed, children were more likely to have a go at answering questions without fear of failure at a higher rate than previously and they were able to better regulate their emotions. During Year 6 school camp, I observed 11 and 12-year-old children using their meditation techniques to overcome their fears whilst navigating high ropes courses and abseiling course. This was a moment when they realised that they can use breathing and other relaxation techniques to overcome difficulties and achieve things they never thought that they could. These are strategies they will now be able to utilise during their lives when things get tough.

My dream is that we can teach all children to go within and find their inner beauty and strength to overcome life's difficulties. I am not opposed to medications, and sometimes children will need the medications to be able to quieten the mind in order to access meditation. The research tells us that meditation is far more effective in the long term than medication, and if we stick with it, it will actually change the physiology of the brain to enable better decision making which the Dunedin project tells us is a predictor of a positive life.

I recall the time that I was raising three teenagers in our house. We had our share of ups and downs. I am sure that there is not a parent in the world that cares too much about getting A's in school over a positive mental attitude and the ability to calm thoughts and navigate the way through adolescence with a health mental attitude. Imagine if we could teach these techniques early on so that children could learn to manage their thoughts and emotions as self-regulate as needed, our suicide rate would start to reverse its current trends.

What can we do?

Relaxation through breathing

"Concentrate your breath until you reach the flexibility of a new-born": Lao Tze, a Chinese sage, described this method of relaxation 2400 years ago!

Breathing is indeed a completely natural and permanent automatism as long as we are alive. We inhale and exhale air without having to think about it and the breathing rate adapts to our body's need for oxygen. However, these needs fluctuate according to our muscular activity. As muscle tone increases, respiratory rate increases. The goal of all relaxation is to lower muscle tone.

Jacobson progressive relaxation

Jacobson was an American physiologist who practiced at Harvard. He developed his relaxation method in 1938 based on the idea that muscle tension would have an effect on thoughts and emotions. Originally, this method aimed to develop proprioceptive sensitivity and refine muscular sense in order to be able to identify and then reduce tension (Larroque, 2013). This learning is done by practicing alternately, for each muscle group, muscle contractions and relaxation; focusing on the different areas of the body one after the other in a certain order, hence the name progressive relaxation: hands/arms, legs, chest/belly, forehead, eyes, throat.

Some authors have spoken of "muscle psychoanalysis". This method lets you become aware of the muscles used in everyday life and learn how to relax to reduce stress and anxiety. Note that this work of discernment of the different muscle groups also makes it possible to realise that no part of the body is totally isolated from the others; for example, it is difficult to contract the muscles of the hand without engaging those of the forearm (Cungi and Limousin, 2006).

In its original version, this method was very long (2 to 3 hours) but it is often used today in abbreviated versions, targeting muscle groups in a more global way.

Schultz autogenic training

This method was developed in the 1930s by Johannes Heinrich Schultz, a neurologist. Schultz was influenced by different currents of thought of his time; let us cite in particular the works of Oscar Vogt on hypnosis, those of Émile Coué on conscious autosuggestion and the notion of the unconscious developed by Freud.

The term autogenic refers to the notion of self-training. It is a technique of concentrative self-relaxation: indeed, it uses both concentrations to perceive bodily sensations of support, heaviness, and heat, but also suggestion and imagery. The suggested sensation is first imagined and the image gradually turns into a real sensation (Larroque, 2013).

Hypnotic relaxation

Hypnosis is a state of rest and the deep relaxation that can be achieved through this method is well documented. Complete physical relaxation corresponds to the hypnoid state, degree 5 of the first stage of hypnosis in the Davis and Husband scale. But hypnosis goes beyond physical relaxation. It is a **state of modified consciousness** different from sleep and allowing a suspension of critical thinking and judgment. It makes it possible to obtain effects, in particular somatic, beyond the reach of the will.

Link between relaxation and meditation

Teaching meditation often begins with relaxation practices that are intended to facilitate meditative practice. However, the goal of meditation, regardless of the approach taken, is not to achieve a state of relaxation, although that is often the effect produced.

Despite their differences, relaxation and meditation are two effective approaches to stress management. While in relaxation, the intention is to relax the body, using different exercises or mental imagery, in meditation (Mindfulness in particular), it is a question of experiencing the present moment in an attitude of observation and no judgment. However, meditation is more likely to reduce ruminations and distracting behaviour and thoughts (Jain et al, 2007).

Let's Talk about Childhood Trauma

In recent times we have become more educated on the impact that childhood trauma can have on each of us throughout our lives. Dr Gabor Mate talks about "Big T" trauma and "Little T" trauma. Big T trauma are the big events that can impact our lies such as adoption, the death of a parent, abuse of any kind, etc. and Little T trauma are the small things that can have a lasting impact on us such as bullying by others, comments made by teachers or parents etc that can cause us to have lasting negative perceptions of ourselves.

If you have experienced childhood trauma, it may be surprising that these distant issues have an impact on your adult life. You may think that if you are not happy in your life today, it is because these traumas are not healed, and today, you don't know where to start to free yourself from it.

My Personal Experience

There are a number of well-known scenarios that contribute to childhood trauma including abandonment, abuse and death of a parent. I experienced 2 out of 3 of these. I was born to a 20-year-old mother and 18-year-old father. Neither parent was in the position to care for a child and the relationship was not one that was going to last. My biological mother was training as a nurse in a Sydney hospital. In the 1970's is was not socially supported or acceptable to raise a child as a single mother, especially if you were from a Catholic family. My biological mother was sent to a Catholic home for pregnant women. She stayed there until her waters broke, in church, of all places and she gave birth to me. I was then placed on foster care whilst a suitable family was located. Research has now discovered that children who are removed from their mothers at such an early age begin to feel a sense of abandonment as the mother is not available to fulfil the child's needs. The child can qui9ckly develop a sense that they are unworthy of love and having their basic needs met. When became a mother, I understood the importance of building connections with my children in those early stages of life. As an adult I understand that the choices my biological parents made were out of love for me however the blueprint was already created. I was adopted into a beautiful family who were unable to have children of their own. I had a mum, dad and older brother. Things were starting to go well!

Unfortunately, the day after my seventh birthday, my life would change again. I remember the beautiful dolly varden cake my mum had organised and the friends that had come to my place for my birthday party. I know mum had been sick and she needed to lie down during the party. Dad took her back to hospital that night and my brother and I were taken to one of a number of caring neighbours to be looked after. I remember dad coming to collect us in the morning and he was talking to the babysitter. The babysitter started crying and tried to hide her tears from me as I greeted my father. Once we were home dad broke the news that our beautiful mother had died that night. Although I knew she was sick, I never expected that it would be the last time I felt her warm hugs or felt that kind of pure unconditional love.

Life for me was then very different. Dad was a coal miner who would leave for work at around 5.00am. At 7.00am he would call the home phone and my 8 year old brother and myself would get up, make our breakfast, get ready for school, walk to the bus stop and come home at the end of the day and wait for dad to get home. We had a lot of time on our own. To make things easier in the morning, one of the relatives had decided that they would cut my hair really short because I didn't have anyone to help me put it in pretty pony tails like the other girls, I also started to gain weight as I made my own "bad" food choices before and after school, and I started to get bullied for my appearance at school. I was the fat kid with the bad haircut. These things stick and create wounds that take a long time to heal and added to my sense of unworthiness and unlovability.

Dad found happiness again a few years later and remarried. This was great for us as a family but it did come at a cost. We were never allowed to speak my mum's name again as it would have been disrespectful to mention her as we had a new mum now. It is not that easy to change mums. I know it is not easy for people to take on step children either and again the psychology of my childhood was the "I don't fit", "everyone I love leaves me", "I am not worthy of happiness".

These scars take a long time and dedication to work through. I took many risks throughout my life with the attitude that "I don't care, people don't stick around" and I pushed people away.

Proudly, I have been married for 30 years now, no matter how hard I pushed, my beautiful husband never left and has always been by my side cheering me on and loving me so deeply. It did become easier to accept his love once I started to accept and love myself. I initially could not believe that this handsome man would want to be with me. Remember, I was still the fat kid with the bad haircut in my own head. I was pregnant with our first son prior to our marriage and convinced myself that he was only with me because I was pregnant. When he didn't leave me once our son was born, I believed that I needed to be better for him to stay and love me. I thought that if I worked really hard and earnt a decent salary he would stay if for nothing else, the quality of life we would have. By the time I was 25 I had three children, was working 4 days per week and completed a psychology degree. I was appointed to my first Principal position at the age of 29 and three years later started a PhD. I worked really hard to contribute to our family finances so that we could build a comfortable life so that he would stay. Although teaching does not pay as well as corporate career, I was determined to climb the salary ladder as quickly as I could.

When I was hit by the car in 2014 and I was unable to work as a principal, he stayed... I had to reconsider my thinking about our relationship and finally accepted that he loved me for me and was not going to leave. No matter where we lived, if I made money or not, he was on this journey we call life with me by his side. He could not understand why I would think any different. It is the scars of the past that contribute to our sense of self and our relationships. I had to reconcile my own childhood trauma to fully understand its impact on my personal reality and the way that I interacted with the world around me.

Maybe you haven't been feeling well lately, and you're wondering, *"Am I suffering from unresolved childhood trauma?"* You might have had the feeling that all this was behind you, and yet, you are experiencing current difficulties and you say to yourself *"Why now?"* You might be experiencing symptoms of anxiety, panic or even a depressive episode for no apparent reason. You might begin to retreat from your life and stop doing the things that make you happy. How could your childhood trauma be unresolved? And first of all, what is all this about?

Unresolved childhood trauma

Perhaps you might have heard this term before but, you may not exactly know what 'unresolved childhood trauma' actually represents. You have been telling yourself that what belongs to the past is the past and that you have moved on but this is simply not the case. In many cases, people have undergone therapies as well however, they still continue to suffer.

Children who have been traumatised have it deeply written in their minds, their memories, their emotions, in their body, in their energy. These memories, even if they are unconscious or rebuffed, are etched within your symptoms, your low self-esteem and your struggle with relationships. Traumatised children have often considered themselves to be alone and do their best to make out things on their own. Now, the issue is that not much can be done on your own. This is the primary and the deepest reason as to why childhood trauma remains unresolved.

You might then ask yourself, "Even though I went to therapy?"

Unfortunately, yes. Many therapists are not experts in childhood trauma. There is no pattern, because your experiences and your pains are unique, and need special treatment to free you from them. The roots of your childhood trauma, unfortunately, remain unresolved. Symptoms might remain hidden for some time. But stress associated with emotional upheaval, or an event that serves as a too close reminder of your earlier trauma can bring you back to the original experiences.

How does this affect you as an adult?

These traumas linger because often, no matter how hard you tried to keep going, there is still a traumatised child living inside of you. If you haven't had enough help or the right therapy to resolve it, your inner child is still hurting. You may not feel it on a daily basis, but remembering it when you are living resonates with that unresolved trauma. Depression, anxiety, panic attacks, eating disorders, obsessive worries, catastrophic anxieties and relationship fears are all symptoms that something lingers inside you. You may have difficulty trusting, low self-esteem, fear of being judged, constant attempts to please, outbursts of frustration, or symptoms of social anxiety that won't stop.

Generational trauma by Dr Gabor Mate

Trauma is the invisible force that shapes our lives. It conditions how we live, how we love, and how we make sense of the world. It is the root of our deepest wounds. Dr Maté offers us a new vision: a society aware of its trauma in which parents, teachers, doctors and administrators do not focus on controlling behaviours, diagnosing, treating symptoms and making judgments, but rather seek to understand the sources from which arise troubled behaviour and disease in the wounded soul of the human being.

We could undoubtedly say that all this can be determined by the style of education and the educational scheme, without forgetting the weight of memory and of that conscious or unconscious narration that encompasses all family dynamics. The one, thanks to which the past continues to be present by different means. On the other hand, it is something that goes beyond, something that, as we have already mentioned, can occur at a genetic level.

The concept of generational trauma was carried forward by Dr Masaru Emato who questioned the impact of time factor in generational trauma. Dr Emoto's experiment consists of taking three jars of rice and addressing them in three distinct ways: the first will receive love and gratitude, the second, contempt and negativity, finally, the last will not be entitled in any way and will be totally ignored. Result: only the first jar begins fermentation, the second darkens, and the last begins to rot. The scientific community will decry this experiment because its protocol methodology does not meet community standards.

From the work of Dr Emoto to the theory of John Bowlby

However, I note that this observation echoes the theory of attachment developed by the psychiatrist and psychoanalyst John Bowlby. The concept presented focuses on the impact of short- and long-term separations from the mother as well as in the deficiencies of maternal care. No, the mother is not guilty of everything. Anyone can give love, but we have to face the facts: she still often plays the role of 'first love giver' while fathers are still attached to their position of 'chronic deserter.' Everyone knows how babies are made, but no one knows how dads are made, as the artist Stromae reminds us.

Being separated from our own mother at birth or during the first months resulting in lack of affection can be disastrous for the child. Even if we are not aware of it and we minimise it with the time barrier, our body remembers it. Persuaded with or without words of love, the body takes note. Although most of us have few memories of our very first years, our body has registered any manifestation of love but also of lovelessness or absence of love. An interesting illustration of this postulate is the story of Doctor Mate.

The lighting of doctor Gabor Maté, specialist in addictions

Hungarian-Canadian doctor holding specialisation in the treatment of addictions, Dr Gabor has claimed that any psychological disorder or chronic illness has its origins in childhood trauma.

Till the trauma emerges in the limelight, the body carries traces of it, its symptoms, placing you in a very uncomfortable and unbearable position. Such a situation has always been a breeding ground for addictions that offers a temporary illusion of evaporating discomfort and the unbearable. Some end up sick, others in prison.

He uses his personal history to explain his analysis. As a baby, he kept crying and his mother was distraught. She consulted a paediatrician who explained to her that there was nothing to be done: all the Jewish babies were crying. As you will have understood, Dr Gabor, of Canadian and Hungarian nationality, was born during the Second World War. The mother's distress was palpable for her child, even intrauterine. A baby feels everything. Subsequently, she was forced to abandon him s for some time to save his life. Doctor Gabor grew up developing strong addictions and an attention disorder, diagnosed late at age 53. It is by looking into his own addictions, in particular work and shopping, that he will make the link between his childhood trauma and his disorder. For him, it is a consequence of the stress suffered from his first months. In this case, the absence of words and affection generated evils.

After the absence of words, there are the verbal banalities with the aftertaste of torture

If I had to choose between physical violence or verbal violence, I would prefer to be beaten, without hesitation. The marks are visible, we can at least complain. Everything that is said, it drives you crazy. Wounds are invisible. Nobody takes care of it. Real bruises heal a hell of a lot faster than insult marks. (Testimony taken from the book "Toxic Parents" by Susan Forward)

Although there is no doubt about the existence of psychological sequelae following physical violence, this testimony highlights the intensity of the verbal sequelae. This stems from their invisibility which is equivalent to their inexistence in the eyes of the world and especially in the eyes of the enunciator or the enunciator. *More words, always words, the same words*, sang Dalida. Psychotherapist Susan Forward explains that they are like mental and emotional seeds that grow within us. On the one hand, there are the 'good seeds' of love, respect and independence, and, on the other hand, the "bad seeds" imprinted with fear, obligation and guilt. *Magic words tactical words. that ring false.* The nastiest one's sound innocuous and are usually pronounced with treacherous 'it's for your good' packaging.

Narcissists' words with perverse long-term effects

The words we say on a regular basis have a deep impact during childhood. A child does not know how to protect himself as humans' game. Humans are the only incapable and dependent mammals when they arrive on Earth. The animals themselves, after only a few hours of life, get up, walk, eat and drink. Just watch the video on the work of ethologist Konrad Lorenz, which inspired psychologist John Bowlby, to realise the status of "God" that parents have and especially the mother. The first moments after the chicks hatch from their eggs are crucial. Those who are in need of attention, you know what you have to do.

Like Gods, parents' words are all-powerful and can have unsuspected destructive effects. The children, like thirsty baby birds, drink in the words of the parents while not yet having the power to detect the poison.

A child constantly criticised with few signs of affection will have low self-esteem and will have difficulty in undertaking. The child will always feel, wrongly rather than rightly, the prey to criticism. The impression that the world is against him. A child mocked under cover of humour "you're a nothing" or a more common "you're really dumb" can be fatal.

"Children take sarcasm and humorous exaggeration at face value. They do not have enough social experience to

understand that a parent is joking which is sadistic and a destructive way." (Susan Forward)

An example of transgenerational trauma

Andréa suffered sexual abuse from a family member for much of her childhood and adolescence. She grew up in an unstructured environment in which her mother was also abused during her childhood. Once she was able to get out of this scenario, having reached adulthood, she refused to receive psychological support to deal with this trauma. *She just wanted to forget, to turn the pages as quickly as possible.*

The imprint, the wound, remained buried in her and expressed itself through various means: anxiety, eating disorders, low self-esteem, hyper-vigilance, depression, insomnia... To this we add a fragile immune system, with weak defences that make her vulnerable to infections, flu, allergies...

Andrea now has a 7-year-old boy. It's her reason for living and her whole world, she found stability and strength in him, in addition to a reason to take better care of herself. On the other hand, she realises that raising her child is more and more complicated: he sleeps badly, has attention problems, many tantrums and difficult behaviours. When called from his school, Andréa has the feeling that her role as a mother is questioned. This feeds into her anxiety and other mental health conditions. She unwittingly has raised her child in a state of her unresolved trauma. She has passed this on. Even though he has not been exposed to the sexual abuse, he has been exposed to the trauma surrounding this which Andrea has left unresolved.

The family: first encounter with authority

The family is the first environment for socialisation with an authority figure. When the latter is dysfunctional, the child will have integrated the dysfunction as being the norm. They have never been invited to discover themselves, to be fully. Lovelessness or lack of love has been interpreted as a consequence of the child's behaviour. The child then feels responsible for these words. If his parents have this attitude, it is probably that he has committed a fault. From there, the child will adopt compensatory behaviours—often addictions—which will also build an armour or shell that will give him or her the capacity to bear the intolerable. An often-observed strategy: get good grades everywhere to be liked or avoid going to boarding school.

Dr Gabor describes the personality of these individuals as a sum of defence mechanisms and not their real identity, hence a certain void that addictions come to fill. In truth, these traumatised individuals have little or no idea of their true identity since they were never allowed to be who they are.

They are then fragile individuals, without a backbone. Only, to face injustice and abuse, you have to be able to stand up and set limits. However, these individuals have been accustomed to restricting themselves to the limits of others and expect limits to be placed on them. They are not sovereign of their life. They are then at the mercy of any authority – good or bad. Often, it also happens that these people are stuck in a narcissistic phase thinking that they are responsible for what happens to them. They desperately seek the attention and love they never received when they arrived in this world.

The other side of the coin is often loneliness and misunderstanding. Because they are unable to relate. When these beings become parents, the tortures begin. In a way, their interest will prevail. For these individuals, parenting will be a way to get the attention and love they have never experienced. The height being their inability to receive and express it. Therefore, their love becomes, in most cases, a conditional love. In this type of situation, the children should detach themselves from it. In the best case, the parents will have worked on them and will not repeat these patterns. **Nevertheless, this reality will be rarely—or belatedly— detected as the illusion of a healthy family pattern is powerful.**

When childhood patterns come to work: exhaustion, unstable career, burnout

When the parents have not done this work, and the illusion persists, the children wear the consequences unconsciously. This can result in professional situations that have become "classic" with, on the one hand, deeply narcissistic hierarchical superiors anchored in the ego driven by their need for recognition; and on the other, employees with the same weaknesses. The latter will respond to this "bad" authority by giving themselves without limit, by simple mimicry of the known family pattern. These are comparable to hungry people unable to feel satiety because they have never experienced this emotional satiety.

The satisfaction of the parents or the employer becomes an illusory trophy which brings them closer to their original emptiness until the day of the drop of water. Like a film that can no longer last, the spotlights go out, black imposes itself and pushes us behind the scenes. The script no longer sticks. It rings false. This no longer makes sense and it has become impossible to restart the machine. You have to rewind to understand. Watch the movie from the beginning. Scene by scene. The most memorable but especially those that have been forgotten because they are too difficult. Those that we preferred to put under the rug but whose body always undergoes the weight of more and more pressure.

Like an emotional anaesthesia, the ego and the subconscious erased these images to protect us. As the healing process begins, the memories slowly come back. The light is on and we are strong enough to welcome them. The evils subside, we put words on our feelings, our sufferings. We break the invisible chains that we did not want and that we could not see. This joins the phenomenon of traumatic amnesia which affects many victims of sexual abuse. Memories suddenly resurface after twenty, thirty or even fifty years later.

Obviously, the dysfunctions of the parental schema will impact the sentimental plane in the same way, where co-dependency will surface. Like a drug addict, the traumatised becomes attached to the source of love in an irrational way and often multiplies unsatisfactory relationships. Worse, he does not find himself face to face with a being with the same wound.

Accepting the existence of evils: mourning the old "me"

This process of inner investigation confronts us with the following conclusion: I have never been myself...who am

I? Of course, some parts of your personality were expressed but a large part was missing.

There are said to be five stages of grief: denial, negotiation, anger, depression and acceptance.

1. **Denial** because until then, we thought we were in control of our lives, we managed, as best we could. We reassured ourselves with phrases such as "All families have turbulent times and a past".

2. **Negotiation** because we tell ourselves that somehow it's not their fault (and it's true) and we still want to play the role of the manager. Superman or Wonder woman.

3. **The anger** because we realise that they could have thought before having children and traumatised them. Rest assured, a study has established that three out of four children are unwanted (timing, accident, relationships without original attachment...).

4. **Then comes depression** because deep down, we are in pain and we have never understood it. It is a silenced pain that must be expressed, VERBALISED. We have the right to have pain. To cry in silence, to regret his childhood. We unconsciously punished ourselves with unhealthy compensations.

5. **Finally, salvation**, acceptance because we realise that deep down, we are a human being with qualities, often minimised, and that it is up to us to cultivate them. We learn to be that parent to ourselves through the mistakes of our parents.

If there was a quote to remember in connection with this subject, here it is: "The more sorrow digs into your heart, the more love can enter it."

The origin of evils and words: the transgenerational, an overview

In 1995, the paediatrician Thierry Joly wrote about the family, "It is within it that we observe the first ill-treatment reserved for children, whatever their socio-economic and cultural level. And this first mistreatment does not necessarily reflect a lack of love, but often the inability to know how to manifest this love. It is true that we only transmit easily what we know well. So, it's not that the parents don't like you, they do like you. You are not immune: It is often difficult not to fall back into repetitive family behaviour, into spirals of error. We risk subjecting our children to the same excesses that we blame our parents for it is difficult to fully master the words and gestures of love when one has not oneself been the beneficiary."

This is why we must be vigilant and not take repetitive behaviours or situations in our lives lightly. When something repeats itself, there is something to understand. By daring to shed light on our patterns, we have the power not only to soothe our lives but also those of those around us. A human being at peace with his or her story will be at peace with his neighbour, his wife, his man, his boss and his child. A tool for signing the armistice is probably the last work entitled "The key to your energy" by Natacha Calestreme.

By educating your children with love and kindness, you literally change the world

Dr Gabor goes further by explaining that the decline of today's society is correlated with these traumatised human beings fleeing their deep wounds. Whether it is the lure of gain, attention or power, these three illusory quests are only a way to fill an inner void that has never been identified. As a result, addictions abound and allow consumerism to reign, praised by the inaccessible star represented by exponential and perpetual economic growth. This also joins the conclusion of Dr Joly in the 1990s who already said that "it is probably not knowing how to communicate effectively that makes our society so sick. I would add that it is certainly not knowing how to LOVE that makes our society so sick."

In conclusion, parents or future parents, or simple individuals in contact with children: Turn your tongue seven times in your mouth before speaking. Sow seeds of love, respect and independence in their minds. With your words, you have the power to avoid many evils for future generations, what I am saying is for all of humanity!

Conclusion (And a Bit Cheeky)
Mindful Meditation is the New Sexy!
Your thoughts and feelings create your reality
– Dr Joe Dispenza

Sexy?

How can meditation be sexy?

Have you ever met someone you thought "glowed" from the inside? How attractive were they?

Each of us can improve our attractiveness and hence our sexiness by glowing from the inside.

Mindful meditation as a way of living has proven to be a successful strategy to achieve this. People who meditate tend to look younger (sexy) are more present (sexy) make you feel important in their interactions with you (sexy) demonstrate kindness (sexy), are more creative (sexy), have a real sense of who they are which means they have no desire to pull others down (sexy!), have more fun (really sexy!), love more (sexy), laugh more (sexy).

I hope to have inspired you to give mindful meditation a go so that you too can learn these secrets to improved health, wealth and happiness in your daily life.

If we can pass this gift onto the next generation. We could improve their overall mental wellbeing and produce happier, more resilient children.

Let's practice FARKing so that we don't FUCK up our children. Yes, **F**un, **A**we, **R**elaxation and **K**indness.

Fun

Find opportunities for fun. We live in a world that is increasingly taking away the fun. I am not talking about having fun by teasing others or at the expense of another person's self-esteem. I am talking about opportunities to really enjoy ourselves. Dance like no one is watching. Really, if you are the only person not dancing you are standing out more than the ones who are doing it badly but still enjoying themselves!

Find a hobby that makes your heart sing. You will probably meet some like-minded people if you join a group, that will become lifelong friends. Take time out for fun activities. Life does not have to be all work and no play. There is no fun in being the "richest man/woman in the cemetery" with no one to share it with whilst on Earth.

Be like Sir Richard Brandson. Make fun a priority each day. Look for opportunities to laugh and make others laugh. Even if you do not have a great sense of humour, you can develop a sense of fun. People will be more attracted to you if they can sense that you enjoy life. Misery loves company, so if you are looking to brighten your life with happier people, you need to develop these traits in yourself. Read books on how to relate better to others, watch comedy that appeals to you, it might give you some material you can use in your interactions.

People who make time for fun are much happier people!

Awe

Live your life in awe. Notice the absolute beauty and wonder that is all around us. Take the time to consider the wonders of our world, the amazing thing we call life. The absolute power that exists inside each of us. We are all more powerful than we think and the ability to create an amazing life is within us all if we just take the time to find it and take small steps toward our dreams.

The world is filled with awe and wonder. There is so much that is still untapped and undiscovered. The power we hold within us as humans is both scary and breath-taking. We have only scratched the surface of what we can do. This power is not reserved for the rich, the smart or the good looking. The power is in all of us, no one is special enough to be excluded.

I challenge you to think about living a life that you would be in love with. What job would you have? How would you relate to friends? Who would your friends be? What would your relationship look like? How abundant would you be? Where would you live? Now have a go at one of the meditation techniques discussed in this book or one of your own. Meditate on this life that you love as if you are living it now. Stick with it each day and begin to notice, with awe, the incremental changes that are occurring to bring you into alignment with the life you can fall in love with. Now that would be really sexy, to wake up each morning in love with life!

Relaxation/ Meditation

Take time to relax. The phone calls can be delayed a bit and the work can wait for a few hours whilst we unplug and relax. Give meditation a go! As the science is made more accessible about the benefits of meditation on our minds and bodies it will be undeniable that it is worth each of us persisting to make the effort to "do nothing" and tap into the unknown that exists for all of us to heal and live a happier, more mindful life.

Relax and meditate with your children as soon as you can. The earlier we teach them the strategies to calm themselves and control their thoughts and manage their emotions, the easier it will become for them. They will know the strategies to call upon when things get difficult. If you have ever raised teenagers, you will know how important their happiness and mental health become. Imagine if, in your family you could send your children to their room for some time within instead of time out. If you could give them the opportunity to meditate and reflect on their behaviour, or visualise the outcomes they want to any scenario. The ability to go within and manage their thoughts and emotions can be a lifesaver for many. When things get dire and they lose the will to move forward in their lives, the ability to imagine a different reality and take a step toward this, however slowly, might be a game changer for many. For me, as a parent, I wish happiness first and foremost for each of my children. There are many examples people can raise where money and fame have not brought happiness and in fact many billionaires would at times love the quiet life to simply relax, have fun and live in awe, but they are wired to earn more money. In many cases they believe that the money and power will fill a void, but it never does. The happiest people I know have been able to attract the abundance they desire, but the root of their happiness in their connection with themselves and the world around them. Just as misery loves company, happiness and inner peace attracts more of the same, it is the law of the universe. This does not mean that happy, positive people do not suffer hardship. The difference is that these people have the strategies to cope with such scenarios. They are able to put issues into perspective and move forward, learning from the past and building a better future.

The meditation project that I described earlier with children demonstrates that meditation does impact mindfulness and happiness. The fact that the biggest change in behavioural and emotional difficulties occurred after six weeks of regular daily meditation could strengthen the research that suggests that as adults it takes eight weeks of consistent daily meditation to thicken the prefrontal cortex and reduce the amygdala. The pre-frontal cortex is our rational brain that helps us to keep calm and carry on. Our amygdala is our fear centre. Our research with children suggests that the child's brain plasticity may allow this to occur earlier and is worth further investigation. Teachers noticed that children in classrooms around the four-week mark were more inclined to have a go at answering questions they were not sure they would get right. This could be due to the reduction of the fear cells in the amygdala. Again, more research is worth pursuing.

Imagine if the first recommendation of our child psychologists and paediatricians was meditation, time in nature and quality family time to overcome mental health issues rather than medication.

Kindness

Be kind to yourself and others. It is easy for us to show kindness to others and try to help them overcome their difficulties, but it is not so easy for us to be kind to ourselves. In fact, if we can be kind to ourselves, we are going to be far better coaches to our loved ones. Not one of us it perfect! We all make mistakes, we all feel shame, embarrassment and guilt at various times throughout our lives.

Kindness is something that we are all capable of. It is easy to be kind to others, in fact the endorphin rush can make it as addictive as the best chocolate (I am loving the Belgium kind at the moment). When we carry out a random act of kindness for others it is our reward also. The hardest thing about kindness is to show loving kindness to ourselves. We can easily help others to see their way out of a difficult situation and encourage them to forgive themselves or let go, but it is far more difficult for us to do that for ourselves. Just like meditation, we need to practice loving kindness for ourselves. Once we love and forgive ourselves we are more able to be there for others. We need to hold kindness in our own hearts to be able to receive it from others. When we can love and forgive our past, reconcile our childhood trauma and understand ourselves and our reactions we can begin to heal. This healing is the best gift we can give to our children so that we do not pass on the generational trauma but rather turn it into generational healing.

The best gift we can give to our children is our own happiness. Once we are happy, it liberates our children to find their own. We owe it to the next generation to do better. Let's all take steps forward each day to heal and find happiness so that we can begin to heal our world.

The last words go to Whitney Houston:
I believe the children are our future
Teach them well and let them lead the way
Show them all the beauty they possess inside…

Because the greatest love of all
Is happening to me
I found the greatest love of all inside of me!